"In graceful, measured pros
emotions, Jeremy Tiang pro
identity. Home and abroac
characters' search for their
both universal and thorough
the arrival of an important writer."
—Tash Aw,
author of *Five Star Billionaire*

"The quietude and elegance of Jeremy Tiang's words almost belie
the true power of his prose. These carefully observed stories defy
categorisation—they are Singaporean only as much as they are
trans-global only as much as they are post-national—and implore
us to reconsider our identities in their (and, by extension, our)
oblique exactness. A class act."
—Amanda Lee Koe,
author of *Ministry of Moral Panic*, winner of the
2014 Singapore Literature Prize for Fiction

"An engaging and penetrating examination of the Singaporean
psyche, at home and abroad."
—Dave Chua,
author of *The Girl Under the Bed*

"With characters that are immediately familiar, and situations that
manage to be both ordinary and tragic, *It Never Rains on National
Day* is an incredibly engaging and sometimes uncomfortable
look at belonging, un-belonging and the spaces in between. Once
I started, I could not put it down."
—Tania De Rozario,
author of *Tender Delirium*

"Jeremy's writing is lyrical and soulful, drawing us effortlessly
into the worlds of his many different characters. Grounded
in Singapore but not limited to it, his stories reflect a deeper
yearning for belonging and human connection."
—Yu-Mei Balasingamchow,
co-author of *Singapore: A Biography*

IT NEVER RAINS ON NATIONAL DAY

STORIES

Jeremy Tiang

Copyright © 2015 by Jeremy Tiang
Author photo by Oliver Rockwell. Used with permission.
Cover Illustration by Yong Wen Yeu

Published in Singapore by Epigram Books
www.epigrambooks.sg

National Library Board, Singapore
Cataloguing-in-Publication Data

Tiang, Jeremy, 1977-
It never rains on National Day / Jeremy Tiang.
– Singapore: Epigram Books, 2015.
pages cm

ISBN: 978-981-4655-64-4 (paperback)
ISBN: 978-981-4655-65-1 (ebook)

I. Title.

PR9570.S53
S823 -- dc23   OCN914402886

First edition, September 2015
Third printing, February 2019

for DAH, because because because because

"Thresholds are safe, but unfortunately you can't stay on them for ever."

—Kate Atkinson,
Behind the Scenes at the Museum

Contents

Sophia's Honeymoon

NICHOLAS AND SOPHIA plan their honeymoon by a process of elimination. Not America—Sophia went to college there. They covered most of Asia during their brief courtship. Africa and South America will be perused later, at leisure. Australia is, of course, not even in the running. This leaves Europe, which to Sophia means expensive chocolates and the novels of Thomas Mann.

Thanks to an adolescence of ski trips and inter-railing, Nicholas is already au fait with Europe—not, like many of his fellow Englishmen, cut off from the continent. He speaks French, he likes to boast, with a Parisian accent. Gallant, though, he proclaims that having his young wife with him will make each place brand new.

And so Sophia finds herself in Zurich, a town on a lake. She is astonished to discover such power and influence reposing in a place smaller by a factor of ten than Singapore! There is nothing to match the tall buildings of her own country—everything is faded, wanly charming, like old Christmas cards. She stops taking photographs after realising she is unable to distinguish one picturesque street from another.

This is the first chance she has had to breathe in quite a while. She thought too far ahead, saying yes to the proposal—to the babies, the commitment, the mortgage. The immediate consequence was, in fact, months of flurry as the wedding coalesced around her. Her mother swung into action, not once mentioning her annoyance at her daughter marrying outside their race. In gratitude, Sophia submitted to the cake-tastings and gown-fittings, starting a machine that would not turn off until it had deposited her, winded and flushed, at the altar—where Nicholas awaited her, startlingly attractive in his new Hugo Boss suit.

Nicholas is at home in Zurich, a city of bankers. Although he promised this trip would be business-free, people react subtly when he mentions where he works. They pass him cards. They invite him to country clubs or the ballet. Nicholas declines most of them—*Honeymoon*, he whispers, and the men nod conspiratorially—but a handful he has accepted, rolling his eyes apologetically at her.

She should not complain, she knows. This is the world she has married into, and part of her looks at the box seats and casually expensive lunches, and feels that Europe has spread itself before her feet as if she were a Henry James heroine. And of course it is important that Nicholas make contacts—though he himself would prefer these acquaintanceships to be seamless, to happen without obvious exertion on his part.

She knows they make a handsome couple, and this is part of what draws people to them. They radiate success (or he does, and she is part of this success). Nicholas is tall for an Englishman, just under six foot, and blond without being effete. Sophia does forty-five minutes of Pilates every morning, and never eats carbs after six. She knows what shades to wear to set off her honey-coloured skin and straight black hair. They are the sort of couple one looks at and automatically begins imagining their beautiful children.

Sophia has tried asking Nicholas if they could have more of a normal holiday—infusing her voice with warmth and flirtation, luring him into complicity. *Lazy mornings*, she urges. *Shopping*. He merely raises an eyebrow at her, as if to indicate he will not understand. It is borne home that he is no longer wooing her, and her function has accordingly changed.

On their last day in Zurich, Sophia finds herself resenting their quaint hotel room, its carpeting the colour of mould. She chews grimly on a Sprüngli macaron, aware she is being petulant. Ignoring her, Nicholas is getting ready to go out. In a minute, he will snap at her to get dressed, but now he is moving efficiently about the limited space, enacting a ritual. Now, cufflinks. Now, the tie.

They are going to the opera this evening, the guests of Hanspeter—an acquaintance of Nicholas' from business school. He swooped on them and announced that of course they must not miss the event of the season. Everyone has seen it, this opera, that is what one does in the summer in Zurich. He will arrange tickets, his bank always holds a few for every performance.

Nicholas insists on walking to the restaurant. Sophia does not mind, the cobblestone streets and occasional fountains match her idea of Europe so exactly it gives her pleasure just to be amongst them. An elderly lady drops her scarf without noticing. Not running, merely lengthening his stride, Nicholas restores it to her. The woman exclaims theatrically as her husband nods thanks. They look like a tableau from a play.

At the restaurant, Hanspeter orders everyone Zürcher Geschnetzeites, which turns out to be a thick stew made of veal. It would be a sin to leave Zurich without having tasted this. Hanspeter keeps slipping into his native tongue. Even without understanding what is said, Sophia knows that Nicholas's precise schoolboy Hochdeutsch is more pleasing to the ear than Hanspeter's guttural Swiss German.

Hanspeter's thin wife Mitzi kindly asks Sophia questions about herself. *What do you do? Are you in banking also?* She dabs her exquisite mouth with a napkin after speaking, and leans forward, all polite attention. Sophia has practised her answer: *I used to be at Deloitte, and now I'm a consultant.* She has to stop herself saying "just"—"just a consultant."

Sophia—this is Hanspeter, trying to make the conversation general once more—*Why do you not tell us about your Singapore?* Again, Sophia has rehearsed the answer to this, and is able to speak glibly about the heat, the shopping centres, their adorable new flat in Tanjong Pagar with teak furniture imported from Myanmar. She is careful to emphasise how much of a financial hub it is, mindful that Nicholas suspects people of thinking he has relegated himself to a backwater.

Hanspeter glances at his watch, which seems to be the cue for Mitzi to shepherd Sophia to the powder room. They fix their make-up together, and she is obliged to admire Mitzi's handbag snapshots of their seven-month-old. *It is practically my first night out since he has arrived,* giggles Mitzi. *I have been forgetting what this feels like.* When they return to the table, the men are ready to leave. It is part of Sophia's new life that for her, restaurant bills no longer exist.

Hanspeter drives them out to the opera, which is taking place on the lake. They must look gilded, the four of them strolling by the lakeshore in evening dress, but Sophia is primarily worried about whether her heels will slip on the rough flagstone path. Listening to Mitzi chat skilfully about this and that, she is able to relax and talk about their visit to the Gestalt Museum that afternoon.

They are ten rows back from the front, in a little enclosure reserved for corporate guests. Blank-faced attendants in black bring them glasses of champagne. For a while they sit in silence, sipping and taking in the set, which is constructed on a platform arcing out over the lake, gigantic, with just a hint of sunset around the edges causing the water to glimmer.

Sophia belatedly realises she has no idea what the opera is about. She scans her programme—entirely in German. She should have looked up the plot on the Internet. Nicholas would be mortified if she said anything now. The point is the music, not the story, she tells herself.

The first scene is set in a castle, its towers swooping up unnaturally high. There is some kind of party going on, and Sophia allows herself to be diverted by the sheer spectacle of so many people moving in unison, singing over and under each other to make a wall of sound. It is a carnival, a riot— they hoot and lean flirtatiously into one another, hats and masks colliding.

Next to her, Nicholas seems rapt, unmoving. Mitzi is only half-listening (earlier, she confessed to Sophia, with the air of someone unburdening herself, that she does not really care for Verdi). Hanspeter nods his head almost in time with the music. Sophia only vaguely envies Nicholas his childhood of Covent Garden operas and visits to European capitals, but there are times like this when she feels it as an acute lack in her own life.

On stage, a hunchback is capering grotesquely, his ill-fitting clothes at odds with the sleek elegance of court. He is one of those men who would look out of place in any setting. The other characters mock him uneasily, as if they are secretly afraid. Now they cluster about him, now they wheel away and dance a figure. They exchange words in little bursts of notes, and now and then the audience will laugh to show they got a joke. Nicholas nods appreciatively, as he does at a good volley at Wimbledon.

By the first interval, the lake can barely be seen. The stage now feels sinister, crevices appearing that did not seem to be there before. Sophia is profoundly disturbed by the final scene, in which a woman is abducted by a group of masked men. For some reason the hunchback is also present, but with a scarlet cloth bound round his eyes. The coloratura screams of the kidnapped girl slash through the music, beautiful yet horrible at the same time. The hunchback rips off his blindfold and howls.

Then they are on their feet, applauding, and the stage dims as the singers drift away. Someone brings them erdbeerbowle, a concoction of red wine and berries. They half-eat, half-drink it, and soon their lips are tinged with red.

Mitzi flips through her programme, far too well-bred to initiate another conversation with Sophia—it would seem too much like forcing herself upon her. Sophia can feel her strength ebbing, the sullenness return. Glancing at Nicholas' watch, she sees they have only been there an hour.

The seating stands ramp up behind them; there must be close to a thousand people here. They are tall, most of them, and gleam with good health. By her side Mitzi is now, for some reason, singing snatches from the score. She has a light, pleasant voice, and mimics the gestures of the heroine well enough. The men are laughing and applauding her, as if this is a normal thing to do.

It occurs to Sophia that she can simply leave. The singers are filing back onto the stage. She moves against the tide of people returning to their seats. Nicholas mutters something about her foolishness, waiting till the end of the interval to go to the toilet. She decides to be asleep by the time he gets back to the hotel room, and claim the next day to have developed a headache.

It is further back to the city than she remembers, but she knows she will not get lost if she follows the shore of the lake. Zurich feels more alive at night. People meander with the glassy cheer of those on their way from one drinking place to another, and she smiles at strangers in a way that is not possible by day. Men loosen their ties. The city feels slack around the edges. It must be close to Walpurgisnacht, and Sophia would not be surprised to see dancing in the streets.

She contemplates going into a bar, but the thought of standing in the gloom, nursing a solitary drink, is as bleak as heading back to the hotel now. She feels like she did in her first month of college, before she learnt how to make friends, hiding in her dorm pretending to study. Now, she is confident enough of her looks to know she needn't do anything, someone will eventually offer to buy her a drink. She has also learnt that such men are not the ones she wants to feel obligated to.

There is a McDonald's on the next corner. She is quite hungry all of a sudden, and does not have much money—the smallest meal here will set her back ten dollars, almost all she has on her. Amusingly, there is a burger designed specifically for Switzerland—the McEmmenthaler. She orders it and tells the boy, carefully, *Vielen Dank*, relieved when he nods and thanks her in return.

The taste of French fries, she notes, is universal, as are the teenagers lounging on the plastic seats upstairs. She must look ridiculous in her satiny evening dress and elaborate hairdo. Despite the advertising leaning heavily on the use of authentic Swiss cheese, Sophia's meal does not taste significantly different from a regular cheeseburger. She eats a third of her fries before stopping herself.

Back outside, the air has turned crisply cold; Sophia's pashmina is still hanging off the back of her seat at the opera. She turns a corner expecting a fountain that is not there, and realises she is lost. She tries to retrace her steps to the McDonald's but the sloping, angular streets defeat her.

Now the crowds are thicker, louder than before. The bars must be closing. She worries that it is getting too late, and for the first time that evening begins to feel the cold prickling that accompanies a sense of wrongdoing. These days, the tone of admonishment in her head comes directly from Nicholas. She begins to walk faster.

Everyone in Zurich speaks English, of course, but no one appears to have heard of their hotel. She might not be pronouncing the name correctly. *It's on a street near Starbucks,* she cries, resisting the urge to physically grab someone. People shrug and smile apologetically, then move on before they get lumbered with a lost tourist. She cannot help noticing that Swiss men carry themselves as if perfectly proportioned, but are generally on the large side and would be considered fat in her own country.

It begins to feel as if she will never get back to the hotel, or Singapore, or anywhere that could be considered a place of safety. The laughter of strangers now sounds sinister, and she stumbles more than once on the picturesque cobblestones. At some level, she knows that girls like her are always rescued eventually, but there is no immediate way out of her situation. She walks past dark shop windows and unfriendly houses. There are no signs, nothing telling her where to go.

Many years later, Sophia will think of this night, and how close she was to tears. She will wonder how she could have allowed herself to arrive there, but also feel a twinge of loss for the girl still capable of losing control. Her feet sore and her chignon unravelling, Sophia cannot be expected to take a broader view; she is too busy fighting the rising panic to see that this might be the last moment she is fully herself.

She feels a sudden touch on her elbow, and looks up to see Nicholas. His suit is immaculate, his face well-bred, impassive. *He isn't angry*, she thinks, *I'd know if he were angry*. She can find nothing to say to him. Her wrinkled dress smells of fried food. There is a ketchup stain down her front. Nicholas wraps an arm around her waist and leads her away. He mutters something about nostalgie de la boue, but without any particular emotion behind it. She leans into him as they walk down the narrow street. Everything will be all right, now that Nicholas has found her. This time tomorrow they will be in Vienna.

Trondheim

I WAS ON the overnight train from Oslo to Trondheim when I heard another Singaporean voice, which took me by surprise. I had already spent a week in Scandinavia without encountering any of my countrymen. It might have been too early in the year for the inhabitants of a tropical island to venture this far north—it was barely spring, and there was still snow on the ground.

The voice belonged to a young woman of about my age, twenty-seven, who was trying to persuade the conductor that her ticket was temporarily missing. She had a great deal of charm, but was obviously lying. Realising he was unlikely to let her off, she switched to explaining with great fluency that her credit card had been stolen the day before, so there was no use asking her for money.

I hesitated—it was very inconvenient, I enjoyed my solitude and besides, had just come to an exciting point in my book—but finally decided I would have to help, and called to the conductor. I knew very little Norwegian, and his English was far from perfect, but we understood each other well enough for me to indicate that I wanted to pay for her ticket—billett—and hand over a large amount of kroner. Train tickets always cost so much more when you haven't been organised enough to book them in advance.

After that, she felt she had to come and sit with me, even though there were a great many empty seats in the carriage, and I couldn't think of a polite way of asking her not to. She had very little luggage, just a small bag that she swung gracefully into the overhead rack before slouching next to me. She had long hair that stopped me from seeing her face properly.

There was a pause, longer than I would consider polite— so long, in fact, that I had almost gone back to my book— before she said, "Thank you."

"You're welcome." I could feel my voice was a little stiff, and tried to sound friendlier. After all, she was a pretty girl. "Where did you lose your ticket?"

"I never had one." I had suspected this, but felt a little angry that she wasn't even bothering to pretend.

"You didn't have to do that," she continued. "I know you're being a gentleman, but I thought, what could they do? They surely wouldn't stop the train just to make me get off."

"It's not a non-stop train. Didn't you look at the timetable? There's a stop at Lillehammer, at 3.07am."

"Lillehammer!" she laughed. "Why not? I've never been to Lillehammer."

I decided she was a bit crazy, and turned to look out of the window at the snow, which was falling again, in heavy drifts. I knew we must be passing beside a fjord, but it was too dark to see anything except the clumps of falling white, skewed by the wind. We were only just outside Oslo, yet it felt like the end of the world.

Maybe she felt some of the dull loneliness that Norway seemed to be swathed in, or maybe she thought I was angry to have bought a ticket for someone who didn't care where she went, but she started to explain that she'd lost her Rough Guide, and was happy to cross the country by boat and train, looking at pine forests. "Why Trondheim?" she suddenly asked.

"I'm just staying there for a day," I replied. "A chalet in the mountains outside the city. I want to do some skiing, and then another train further north."

"Why?"

I shrugged. "Reindeer. The Northern Lights."

"Why?"

I didn't know what to say to that. Surely no one has ever needed a reason to see the Northern Lights.

"So which are you?" She looked at me appraisingly, her eyes narrowed. "Singaporean or Malaysian?"

"Singaporean."

"I thought so. Civil service?"

I nodded. "Engineer."

"You don't have to tell me. Glasses and checked shirt.

Plus you have two ballpoint pens in your shirt pocket."

I laughed, trying not to sound uneasy.

"You've studied here?" she said, making me feel uncomfortable with the way she was looking at me, as if I were a specimen. I felt like I was once again in the army, and everything important about me could be deciphered from the little tags sewn onto my uniform.

"You've studied here," she repeated, as a statement this time.

"In Norway?"

"In Europe." She gestured impatiently, taking in the whole continent. "Let me guess. London, Imperial College?"

"Wrong," I said, childishly pleased that she was capable of making a mistake. "Munich."

"Government scholar?"

I nodded.

"Your German must be very good."

"It's all right," I said, trying to be modest. "I lived there for four years. That's why I can speak a bit of Norwegian, they're quite similar languages. And you?"

"The same." She smiled, a sad smile that made her look older. "Singaporean, government scholar. Leeds, English."

This didn't surprise me; she had the look of someone who read a lot of storybooks. "So you're not an engineer."

She laughed as if the idea was ridiculous. "No, I'm a teacher. They make all the English grads become teachers."

This was probably true, but then I couldn't imagine what else you would do with an English degree. She didn't look like a teacher, or rather she looked like the teacher who was different from all the others, the one who wore fashionable clothes to school and once a year went bowling with her form class. I decided that all the boys in her class had a small crush on her, and all the girls went to her for boyfriend advice.

Singaporean etiquette suggested that I should ask her which junior college she had gone to, especially as we were about the same age and probably had friends in common, but that conversational route seemed unspeakably boring just then, so instead I asked her how long she had been travelling.

"About ten days, I think." Her brow wrinkled, as if she was searching her memory. "I wanted to go somewhere cold. I found some cheap fares to Germany on the Internet, and I kept heading north. I didn't realise that everything here would be so expensive."

I nodded with feeling, having just paid the equivalent of fourteen Singapore dollars for a sandwich at the train station.

"And I wanted to see a fjord," she said. "I thought it would be like an Ibsen play. Pine forests, despair, cold water. Trolls in the mind."

"I know Ibsen," I volunteered. "*The Doll's House*. About women's rights?"

She looked at me like I was stupid, the same look the girls in JC used to give me when I hadn't heard of the latest boy band, or turned up at Zouk wearing unfashionable clothes. Trying to reach safer ground, I asked, "Which of his plays do you like best?"

She paused before replying. A teacher's pause, designed to make sure the class was quiet and paying attention. "When I was in Oslo, I went to see a play at the National Theatre. It was by Ibsen, *Little Eyolf*."

"In Norwegian?"

"Yes. It doesn't matter, I know the text well enough to follow it. It's about a young couple who have a crippled child, and they blame each other for the accident that caused his injury. They still love each other, but she's from a rich family, and he's obsessed with his work, so they're beginning to drift apart. Then a strange woman comes to visit them. She lures their son into a fjord and he drowns."

"What happens to the parents in the end?"

"They get on with their lives, somehow."

"That sounds a bit tragic."

"He didn't write cheerful plays. Life isn't like that."

"That's why I seldom go to the theatre. So depressing. Why not cheer up a bit? I prefer comedies."

Again, she looked at me like I was an idiot, as if she was tired of explaining things to me. I suddenly felt very angry. Of course she knew more about plays than I did; she was a girl, and a literature teacher. If we were talking about torques and pressure gradients then she would be the one to look stupid.

"I feel like Little Eyolf sometimes. That's why it's my favourite play; I feel like I'm crippled, and nobody understands what I really need. Sometimes I think I should drown myself."

I was starting to realise what kind of girl she was. "You come from a wealthy family, right?"

"We're okay." She looked a bit startled. Maybe I had changed the subject too abruptly.

"And you live in a big house. Sixth Avenue?"

"Toh Tuck. How did you know?"

I nodded, and didn't bother to reply. I had met a lot of girls like her. The pretty ones in the arts stream who giggled and whispered to each other during their Maths lectures, if they went to Maths lectures. In their spare time, they read a lot of Sylvia Plath and wrote indifferent poetry for the school magazine. Knowing where to pigeonhole her comforted but also puzzled me; girls like that don't end up in faraway countries, scamming train fare off strange men.

She looked annoyed that I wasn't answering her question, then threw her hair back and pouted in a way someone must once have told her was quirky. "Do you travel a lot?" was her next line of attack. I felt like I must be gaining status in her eyes; she sounded like she was really interested in me.

"Whenever I can," I replied. "I have a lot of annual leave, and I'll lose it if I don't take it."

"Most people don't go so far away. Everyone I know just goes to Langkawi."

"I want to see every country in the world before I die. I have a big map on my wall at home, and whenever I go to a country I colour it green with highlighter pen. Anyway, aren't you quite far from home yourself?"

"It's different for me." I thought this was patronising of her, but she didn't seem to notice. "I don't really think of Singapore as home anymore. I don't really know where I belong, but I like to be far away."

I could tell that she thought she was being controversial, but I've met a lot of people like her, especially amongst overseas scholars. Some people spend a few years living outside Singapore and then think that gives them the right to criticise everything. I've seen them talking and laughing during the national anthem, making fun of the National Day Parade. Normally I try to avoid these people, but something made me snap at her, more fiercely than I had intended, "Why do you bother living there if it's not your home?"

"I'm bonded," she said. "You must be too. I'll have to keep working for them for a few more years. I don't have a choice."

That was true, of course. I had forgotten that she had said she was a scholar.

"It's a prison," she went on. "I can apply for a transfer to a different school, but I can't get away. I've asked my parents to buy me out, but they need to pay for my brother's studies. He's doing Medicine in Australia."

"It's not so bad being bonded. I quite enjoy it. It's a nice job, the salary's quite okay, and it means I don't have to think. Why spend time worrying what to do? Jobs are all the same anyway. Just work hard and you'll have time to enjoy life afterwards."

She sighed. "I don't mind teaching. In fact, I really like the kids, some of them are my friends on Facebook. But I don't like not having a choice about what I do."

"You knew the conditions when you signed that bond. Didn't you read the deed? Why would you expect them to pay for your studies and then not get anything in return?"

"I was eighteen. Who on earth can think long-term at that age? I just wanted to get out." This must have been an argument she had used effectively before, because she was looking at me as if expecting me to nod and agree. "Do you think little girls dream about becoming teachers when they grow up?"

Something had been bothering me for a while—a vague sense that her story did not quite fit—and now I realised what it was. "You're a teacher."

She nodded. "GP and English Lit. And I'm in charge of the cross-country team." I looked at her dubiously, and she blushed. "I used to like running. Anyway the new teachers always get the unpopular CCAs."

"If you're a teacher, what are you doing here?"

She tried to laugh, but I think she knew I'd worked it out.

"What, who says teachers cannot go to Norway?"

"You said you've been travelling for ten days now, but the March holidays are only one week long. How come you're still here? Don't you have to go back and teach?" I realised I was pointing my finger at her and quickly lowered it, in case it looked like I was accusing her of something.

"I'm not supposed to be here."

"What do you mean?"

"I was supposed to go back four days ago. Nobody knows where I am now; I haven't turned on my hand phone or checked my e-mail. They probably think I'm dead." She laughed her crazy laugh again, and I wondered if she had actual mental problems. "No, they probably think I've run away. Everyone in the school knows how much I hate it there. I'm always complaining in staff meetings. I don't mean to make a fuss, but they provoke me."

"You've run away?"

"AWOL teacher!" She was still making funny noises that could have been laughter, or small cries of pain.

"Are you in trouble?" I found myself saying, aware that I was talking like a character from a film. She didn't seem to hear me.

"I was in Germany first of all. I did A-Level German, so I thought it would be a good place to start. I took the train from one town to another, without any plan, just drifting. When I started to run out of money I knew I should go back, and my week was up anyway. I was in Hamburg, standing by the harbour, looking out towards the Baltic Sea. The sky there seems too big, all sunset, it made me feel like I was lost, like I was nothing. So instead of going home, I bought a ticket on the ferry to Oslo, and then I couldn't afford a hotel so I thought I'd try my luck with this train."

"Are you going to go back?"

"I don't know." She looked impatiently at me. "Don't worry. I'm not going to sit under a bridge and kill myself."

"It's not that," I protested, annoyed that she found me so easy to read. "Your parents must be worried."

She frowned, but was saved from having to reply by all the lights going out just then. The conductor must have finished checking tickets for the whole train, and now we were settling down for the night. Around us the other passengers were yawning, putting their books away, finishing conversations.

We reclined our seats, and opened the hospitality packs we'd been given. These contained a blanket, ear plugs, eye mask and inflatable pillow. I tucked myself in, but didn't use the earplugs or mask—I had the feeling she still had more of her story to tell. My glasses were tucked into my shirt pocket, so she was now just a blurred silhouette against the greater blur of forests rushing past the train windows.

For a while we stayed like this, silent, just the thrum of wheels and sharp splatters as bursts of snow landed against the windows. The carriage seemed to become a single, warm, breathing mass as we sliced through the night, the only human beings for a hundred miles. I felt myself sinking through layers of something dark and thick as people pulled down their window shades and even the moonlight waned.

When she spoke again, her voice seemed deeper, as if she was pulling at something within herself that didn't want to come loose. "I've travelled to so many countries. My family likes taking holidays; ever since I was a small girl, we would go somewhere different every year. Australia or Canada or Korea. One year we went all over Africa. Then when I was a student, I spent all my money inter-railing, all over Europe. I always feel like I need to escape."

I was now starting to feel sorry for her. "You shouldn't run away." I tried to make my voice gentle, so it wouldn't sound like I was scolding her. "Why don't you tell your parents how you feel? If you're really so unhappy, I'm sure they'll help you."

"I talked to them. They told me not to be silly; nowadays you should be grateful that you have a job. Teaching is an iron rice-bowl."

"Maybe you can ask MOE to transfer you to a different school, sometimes a change of environment can make you feel better."

"Can you find a school where I don't have to go for three-hour staff meetings, or spend all my time filling up forms, and all the other teachers don't tell me how I should behave?"

"I'm sure it's not that bad. Maybe you just need to change your thinking?"

She turned away from me a little. "Why do men always think they need to have an answer? It's okay. I don't expect you to solve my problems for me."

We fell into silence again. I had never met a girl like this before; she seemed contained in herself, but behind the stillness she was an open wound. I didn't know what to say to her. Normally when I go out with girls, we talk about movies or food, but I didn't think she would be interested in these things.

Then her voice came again. "You must think I'm very selfish, only talking about myself. Tell me your problems, Calvin Tham."

I wondered how she knew my name—for a moment it seemed like she could really read my mind—then remembered that it was written on the side of my book. I hate people stealing my books; if you write your name down the side, then it's on every page. She must have taken note of it earlier on.

"What kind of engineer are you?"

"I trained as an electrical engineer, but to be honest, I haven't used a lot of that. I seem to be doing mostly admin work."

"Where are you?"

"Ministry of Manpower."

"You tell people what to do."

"In a way, but it's not that simple." I started to explain to her exactly what my job entailed, but the air between us seemed to solidify, and I realised I wasn't sure myself what I did. I tried to remember my working day, but Singapore seemed unaccountably foreign, like a previous life. I had only been sitting at my desk ten days ago, but it was a blur—I didn't know where the last few years had gone. What did I do when I got into work every day? I turned on my computer, checked my messages, then—what? For the next few hours, what? Day after day clicked by in activities I could no longer list. Perhaps I had always been on this gently creaking train in the dark, all my life, and Singapore had only been a dream. At this moment, anything seemed possible.

We stopped at Lillehammer. The conductor passed through, like an angry ghost, roughly shaking awake passengers whose tickets only brought them this far. The lights came on, very dimly, so they had to grope for their luggage as the remaining sleepers stirred and murmured. On the platform, two or three bleak individuals took final drags on their cigarettes before letting them drop, and stumbled on board. I wondered how deranged your life would need to become before you found yourself waiting for a train at three in the morning.

The train started moving again, very gently, gliding at first and then picking up speed. It was not a new train;

the upholstery, like so much of Norway, appeared to have been preserved intact from the late eighties. Unlike our sleek MRT, busily covering short distances with the screech of metal wheels, Norwegian Rail was stolid and dignified, pistons churning, wheels turning steadily and cleanly along fixed tracks.

I readjusted my inflatable pillow and wondered if sleep would take me. Looking across at my companion, I could see from the reflected gleam of her open eyes that she too was wide awake. Out of impulse I whispered, "You should come home."

"Turn myself in, you mean?"

"I'm flying back in three days' time. Why don't you come back with me? We can make up a story for your school, I'll say you were sick, too sick to get in touch with them, and I had to take you to hospital. I'm sure they'll understand."

"You want to lie for me?"

"You can't keep running forever. What are you going to do? You don't have any money."

"You sound like my mum."

"At least call your mum, so she knows you're alive. You don't have to tell her where you are. Do you promise to call her?"

"All right."

"Why won't you come with me?"

"And do what? Go look at fjords, and then head back

to Singapore like a good girl? Tell my students I was sick, check their holiday homework, and then stand behind them at assembly making sure they don't talk or fidget during the principal's speech? I can't, it's like being buried alive."

"Then what will you do?"

"I don't know."

"You're just being spoilt. No one likes their job; why do you have to be so special? You think anyone really enjoys what they do all day? Just try to do your best; if you don't think about it, then time will pass very quickly."

"I don't need you to be angry with me."

"I'm not angry. I'm just trying to help you. You say you feel trapped, but where do you want to be? Life isn't so bad, after all you have a good salary and Singapore is so easy to live in, low taxes and low crime and nice food. Isn't that enough? Where else do you want to be?"

"Anywhere. Anywhere except where I am."

We were in the far north now, dark and cold for half the year. I was prepared for the roads, which would be treacherous, with spiked shoes and a foldable walking cane. I didn't know what she would do when we got to Trondheim. She seemed so utterly unprepared for anything. Even her clothes didn't look warm enough. I hoped she would be able to steal the blanket from the train and use that until she managed to get hold of a waterproof jacket.

I'm not usually the sort of person who talks to strangers

on the train. I've seen people who do it, just sit next to people and ask them where they're going, leading into hour-long conversations. I don't do it, and I had no idea what to say next. Nothing seemed suitable. I shut my eyes and tried to rest. It was almost four in the morning, and we only had three hours before reaching our destination. I didn't think I would feel human the next day if I didn't sleep at least a little bit. I had planned a full day of sightseeing—the cathedral in Trondheim is the largest medieval building in Scandinavia—and I wasn't sure if I would be up to it.

I had almost drifted off when I heard her voice, low and clear. At first I thought I was dreaming it. She was telling a story, maybe to herself, maybe to me. I listened with my eyes shut. She wouldn't be able to see my face in this light anyway.

"I met him in Hamelin, in the town square. I was only supposed to be there for half a day. There isn't very much to see there, pretty houses and a million tourist trap things about the ratcatcher. But it happened that day—"

"The ratcatcher?"

"You know the story? The pied piper of Hamelin."

"Of course. He got rid of all their rats, but they didn't give him the money they'd promised him. So he came back."

"And took away their children."

"Serves them right. They should have paid him."

"So, that day there was a parade in the town, a pageant telling the story, and I stayed to see it. I don't normally like fairy tales, but the costumes were so pretty. Little children dressed as rats, and other children being stolen, then the ratcatcher himself, tall and blond, all dressed in strange clothes. I started watching and couldn't stop. I followed them, and by the time it had finished I'd missed my train."

"Was there another one?"

"Not until the next day. And the hotels were all full because of the parade. I hadn't realised, so many tourists come especially to see it. I walked around for a while wondering what to do next, it was too cold to sleep outdoors, and then I met him in the town square. The ratcatcher. Without the costume he was just an ordinary man, a bit thin, but I didn't know anyone else so I went to talk to him. I told him I enjoyed his performance. He's not really an actor, he just does this, normally he works in the town hall. He had small grey eyes, like a rat's. When I told him I had nowhere to stay, he told me I could come home with him."

She was very soft now, barely audible. "It wasn't even that I found him attractive, but somehow I followed him. When he touched me I didn't ask him to stop, it's been so long since someone touched me. It got dark very early and we stayed in bed for hours. We didn't use anything. I think I might be pregnant."

The train was completely silent now, moving deeper into nothing, into the dark, no sounds at all except the wisps of her voice.

"When I saw him the next day he was older than I thought, the start of a pot belly, his hair falling out. Blond hair thins so fast. He bought me some food and put me on the train. I didn't care where I went. I asked him to buy me a ticket for any city, any city far away from Hamelin. He stood on the platform for a while, with his hands in his pockets, but then he became impatient when the train didn't leave, he just waved and walked away. It's too early to use a pregnancy test, so I'm just waiting. I can't stay still while I wait."

She seemed to expect me to say something, but I had nothing, no words would come into my head.

"I would do it again," she went on softly, almost in my ear. "Even if I had a second chance. I wanted to hurt myself, but instead I made myself feel alive. I can't go back now."

She spoke a little more, about how there's always a price to be paid, and if you try to escape it will be gouged out of you somehow. I stayed still, hoping she would think I was asleep. After a while, I did drift off, though it was an uneven sleep. I thought I heard her weeping during the night, but it may have been some other sound.

When I woke up, the conductor was shaking me and she was gone. We were in Trondheim, a watery sun coming in and lighting her empty seat, abandoned blanket and a few of her long hairs. She had taken some kroner from my jacket; I had expected her to, and had left the money in an open pocket as you would put out food for a stray kitten.

The rest of my holiday was uneventful. I took pictures for my Facebook page, and then came back to work. From time to time I wonder what happened to her, and if she ever made it back. Whenever I'm in my younger cousins' house, I flip through their school magazines, wondering if I'll see her face. So many different English departments. Once, I don't know why, I hacked into the MOE server to see if I could locate her, but this proved impossible because I had forgotten to ask for her name.

Tick

BY THE THIRD day he has pulled a few dozen ticks off the dog. *This place must be infested*, says his wife, and he nods, unsure whether she means their cabin or the entire natural world. There are ticks in the city, of course, but nowhere near this many. It makes him wonder how many dark, crawling creatures might lurk on the forest floor.

His initial idea was total isolation, but the cabin costs nine hundred a week plus tax. The only way to make that work was for both of them to come, and sublet the apartment. His wife was surprisingly upbeat about this, considering she'd have to commute ninety minutes in each direction. *You owe me one*, she said as they packed. *I'll enjoy the leverage.*

She leaves virtually at dawn to get into town for the early-morning class, but still manages to leave him a grudging paper-bag lunch (*Just like Yaddo*, he tells himself). He can see vast dappled trees and hear the breeze swirling their tops, and faces his word processor with fresh hope. Hard to believe six weeks in such surroundings will not produce a masterpiece.

He has been telling people about this for months: the students, his colleagues, the newsstand guy. Partly to make sure he actually goes through with it, but mostly out of an excitement that even he can see borders on the childish. Everyone responded positively, many wishing they could do the same themselves. So many unwritten novels—how many shelves would they take up? Bad enough the published ones. He feels his own irrelevance each time he steps into Barnes & Noble.

There is no Wi-Fi in the cabin, and his cell phone is locked in an office drawer back in the city. How *edgy* to be so completely cut off. He asks his wife not to tell him if anything happens in the outside world, not even nuclear war, or if Harper Lee writes a third book. *Harper who?* replies his wife, so deadpan he almost believes her.

Even without the Internet, there are multiple ways of squandering the day. He invents a game of throwing crumpled paper into a bucket, with an elaborate scoring system for how close to the rim he gets. It will look good when his wife gets home and sees the trash can full of wadded-up paper.

Hours go by as he watches trees from the porch, telling himself he is emptying his mind of the city. Mid-afternoon masturbation leaves him in need of a nap. He rearranges the tins of food they brought from the city in order of expiry date, then plays with the dog and removes ticks from its skin—a particularly good activity for wasting time as new ones appear every hour. The dog is a shih-tzu, fourteen years old and cranky with age. One of its eyes is misted over from cataracts, and beneath its stringy grey coat the skin is flaking off with infection.

His wife has never gotten into his writing. When they were first dating, he would read her fragments of one short story or another, but stopped when he realised her interest was little more than polite. She likes fitness magazines, and sometimes self-help books. What he does all day holds little mystery for her—she views writing a novel as akin to knitting a pullover; go at it stitch after stitch, keeping count, and eventually you end up with something like the picture on the pattern.

He gets used to the low-level hum of anxiety that runs under every minute of not-writing. Not enough to force him back to his desk, just a thrum of worry that says: you will fail at this too. The tone was set from the first day, on which he squeezed out a single paragraph. His average output has been between half a page and nothing at all. After five days, he pastes everything into a single document and calculates that each word cost him a dollar fifty in rent and food—an investment he is unlikely to recoup, given his desultory publishing history. This is not a viable business model.

Day six is a Monday, which they have designated their together day—his wife is a yoga instructor and weekends are her busiest time. With some misgivings, he closes his laptop and they go for a hike. He could claim to be on a streak, and she would understand—but what if he did, and the day drifted away from him anyway? His wife declares she wants to go as far as the first creek on the map. They walk slowly so the dog can keep up, but still he finds himself huffing before they are halfway there. Only a week away from the gym and already his body is thickening. He resolves to start doing push-ups.

Back at the cabin, they bathe the dog in the sink. It hates this ritual, and whines as she lathers it all over with hypoallergenic shampoo. Running her fingers through its damped-down fur, she exclaims again and again as she finds yet more ticks, small black ovals with wiry legs. She passes them to him to flush away, still wriggling. Some of them are engorged with blood, the size of his little fingernail, so distended their black skin looks grey. *Be careful not to pop those*, says his wife. *They're full of eggs*.

By the time they're finished and the dog is dry, he reckons they must have pulled off more than a hundred ticks. The thought revolts him. He frets about being bitten himself, but his wife says not to be ridiculous, ticks don't bite people. *Isn't that how you get Lyme disease?* he counters. *That's deer ticks*, she says, with an air of finality. He is unconvinced, but without access to Wikipedia it is impossible to refute her.

That night they make love for the first time since coming to the woods. He feels unequal to the effort, as if his daytime ennui has followed him to bed, and in the end it is a listless, perfunctory affair. His wife does not seem to mind, and absently strokes the hair on his chest as if it were a pet, before drifting into sleep.

The next day she disappears into the city again, and he puts on a load of laundry at the highest temperature setting—their sheets, the dog's blanket, the many fur-coated towels that are the inevitable aftermath of bathing an animal. The cabin does not have a dryer, and he has to hang them all on the long clothes-line slung between two trees, careful not to let anything touch the ground in case it picks up unwanted life.

He has promised himself to make a new start—even here, away from the city, the power of routine is not to be underestimated. To protect his writing from contamination, he has not brought a single book with him. Now, he is filled with an urge to see words on a page—any words, other than his own. He finds himself rooting in his wife's bag for one of the paperbacks she reads at night, crouched in the bathroom so as not to tempt him. He finds a gaudy volume by someone called Timothy Ferriss, who promises to help him escape the workplace grind. He reads greedily, standing up, careful not to disturb the bookmark.

It is three before he makes it to his desk. At college, he had an elaborate ritual of writing everything in fountain pen on legal pads, and then again on a typewriter, before finally moving on to the word processor. Now, he bangs directly into his laptop, involuntarily clicking word-count every few minutes. Unhealthy, he knows, but he is desperate to see the number tick upward in tiny increments. *Keep putting pennies in the piggy bank*, he hears his mother say, *and sooner or later you'll have a million dollars.*

Once, he had an agent who phoned him impatiently, wanting to know how much he'd written, when she could expect new pages. A couple of unsold novels later, each dragged from his brain with torture implements, he no longer has an agent. *It's a relief just writing for myself, when I feel inspired*, he tells his friends. *If only I weren't so busy…*

The dog yips to be taken outside. He opens the door for it, watching as it waddles to the nearest tree and releases a jet of urine. He is tempted to leave it out on the porch, but there may be coyotes, and deep down he knows this is not an animal that would survive long in the wild.

Back inside, he gives the dog a thorough pat-down for unwelcome passengers. Unlike fleas, ticks are unable to leap. All they can do is cling to stalks of grass until a passing mammal brushes against them. He grudgingly respects them for thriving despite their haphazard mode of existence. It is a long process: brushing through the fluffy, soft coat, looking for flecks of black against pink skin, concentrating on favourite hiding spots such as the base of the tail, the webbing between its toes. The dog tolerates this at first, glad of any attention, and then begins to whine.

That night he dreams that the forest is a carpet of ticks,

black and brown specks, indistinguishable from grains of soil until they stir. Waking, he can still feel their tiny legs against his skin. He brushes his hands over his body; there is an ant on one ankle, nothing more. Somewhere else in the room, the dog thumps vigorously against the floor, probably trying to scratch some hard-to-reach place behind its ear.

The next morning, he says to his wife, *Is it possible that by only killing the ones dumb enough to get caught, we're inadvertently breeding a super-intelligent race of master-ticks?* She grunts in response, not really listening, trying to get her left foot a little further behind her ear. She always claims that yoga grants serenity, but mostly it gives her a pained, red face.

When she has gone, he decides the only way to crack the ice is to sit at the table and not leave until he has typed an acceptable number of words. He brews a pot of the kind of coffee that punches holes in his stomach and then, not even getting dressed, sits at the table in boxer shorts, building up a good rhythm on the keyboard, just a man and his words. He feels a tickle on his leg and glances down, expecting a bug or bead of sweat. It is a tick, red-brown and feisty, halfway up his calf. He stifles a scream, then wonders why he bothered, there is no one for miles around. He crunches it with a fingernail. There is no blood when it pops, which at least means it hasn't fed on him.

It was probably confused by your leg hair, says his wife

reasonably, when he tells her at dinner that night. *I keep telling you not to worry, their jaws aren't strong enough to break human skin.* He can think of several retorts to this, but decides to keep the peace, focussing instead on the meal in front of him: brown lentils and eggplant parmigiana. There is a small health-food café attached to his wife's yoga studio, and she has charmed the owner into revealing most of his recipes.

A day or two after that, he is startled by visitors. *Intruders*, he thinks at first, before recalling the woods are public land. They seem harmless enough, a man about his age in full beard and flannel shirt, and a girl of maybe nine. They are hiking through the woods, their tent half a mile away—would he mind if they sat a few minutes to catch their breath?

He can hardly pretend to be busy—when they appear, he is slumped on the porch swing, rubbing the dog's belly— and in any case is ravenous for company. He recognises these two as fellow city dwellers poleaxed by nature. The little girl twitches at each rustle in the trees, and flinches when a field mouse scampers a few yards from her foot. He offers them iced lemonade and cookies.

They fill him in on the news he has missed—a nuclear accident somewhere, a politician's gaffe, a plague of moths in lower Manhattan. They're still talking when his wife arrives back, or at least he and the man are; the girl has curled up for a nap on the swing. His wife seems annoyed, her greeting somewhat clenched. Still, she doesn't object when he invites them to stay for dinner, nor when their guest reciprocates by offering up the six-pack of PBR he happens to have in his knapsack.

Soon they are splayed across the cushions and rugs, not drunk but loose enough for the fresh air to go to their heads. The dog, out of its mind at the presence of fresh companions, yelps in sharp asthmatic bursts as it lurches from human to human, demanding to have its ears scratched. This is the sort of night for a crackling log fire, but it is far too hot for that. Besides, he would have to chop some wood first, which he'd probably be inept at.

The man turns out to be a sound engineer—which is, what, something to do with music?—and works mostly from home, which is convenient as he home-schools his daughter. He notes the flash of alarm that touches their faces and says, *Don't worry, it's not like that, I'm not one of those religious nuts.* He isn't indoctrinating his daughter about God planting fossils to test our faith. *It's just*—he pauses here to prise open another can—*her allergies. Almost as soon as she was born, they started. We thought she'd have to live in one of those giant plastic bubbles.*

They turn to look at the girl, who seems perfectly healthy, snoring in sweet curls of sound. The dog has settled at her feet, its breathing almost in sync. *It was ambitious bringing her into the woods*, he continues, *but I didn't want her to miss out. I stuffed her full of antihistamines, I guess we'll wait and see. She's been itching all day. I didn't think there'd be much pollen—*

*Perhaps the insects—*says his wife tentatively, and he is about to mention the ticks before realising it might be tactless to compare dog and daughter. Also, ticks are arachnids, not bugs. Their guest is shaking his head, anyway. *She's slathered in insect repellent—fragrance-free, of course—and I made sure she was in long sleeves.*

The conversation drifts towards movies none of them have seen, and the coming week's weather. The dog licks a foreleg determinedly, as if trying to dislodge a particularly bothersome tick. The girl shifts and scratches in her sleep. His wife gets up to put the kettle on the stove. All the beer is gone.

After the second pot of green tea, the man declares he is sober enough to head back to his tent—if the bears haven't eaten it. For some reason they all find this hilarious. Then his wife starts to explain earnestly there are no bears in these woods, and that sets them off again. They wake the girl, who seems startled and unhappy not to find herself in her own bed. The man has to carry the pack across his front so he can piggy-back her.

As they get ready for bed, he says to his wife, *I wonder if I have allergies. If it's something in the air, the food, that's making it so hard for me to concentrate.* She laughs unkindly. *If they had a drug to fix that,* she says, *I'd have given it to you years ago*. He is silent and she goes on, a bit more conciliatory, *Why don't you go back to yoga? It'll help*. He doesn't tell her he only ever joined her class because he'd heard the faculty boys talk about a hot new instructor, flexible enough to get both legs behind her head.

She is normally insistent on the dog sleeping in its designated basket, for discipline, but tonight she allows it on the bed. Too feeble to jump, it yelps until he lifts it, then snorfles happily amongst the blankets, turning in circles to make a little nest. They fall into shallow, clinging sleep until half past five when the dog, in a froth of anxiety, demands to be let down.

A handful of days go by, and he slips past the halfway point of his stay. Now he fancies he can actually sense things leaching away from him. Not just time, a steady trickle of seconds and days, but also money, credibility, talent, even love. He sits grimly before the laptop, stabbing letters on the keyboard, trying not to ask himself who might want to read what he produces. He has an excruciating memory of their last dinner party when, fuelled by two-thirds of a bottle of wine, he held forth about his need to document the crises engulfing their country. *A chronicle of our times*, he slurred. *Someone has to write it. Someone clear-eyed.*

He stays at his post all day, with only one bad stretch when a couple of hours slip into the black maw of Minesweeper. At least he has a respectable slab of text at the end of the day, although reading back he is surprised how unformed it is. But is this incoherence or raw creative power? His finger flirts with the *delete* button, but the day has been a rare triumph and he cannot relinquish its fruits so lightly. Pushing back from his desk, he feels a satisfactory pain across his shoulders, the aching accomplishment of a day's labour.

His wife is subdued at dinner, and he wonders if he has said something wrong or if she is simply growing tired of him, but then she says, *Sorry, I've had a bitch of an afternoon.* He feels a hot wash of guilt at not having asked, and listens hard as she tells him about her demanding students. When she asks about his day, he shows her the block of text but says he's worried about structure. For a moment as they do the dishes together they seem like a normal couple.

Before bed, she gives the dog a massage. *I suppose it's had a hard day too*, he jokes. She ignores him, running her hands in slow, steady strokes over the thinning grey fur, the white blaze at its crown. The dog groans happily, either at the pleasure of human contact or because she really is relaxing its muscles. Whenever her probing fingers encounter a tick, she briskly removes it between her nails and deposits it on a Kleenex. When the sheet gets too crowded he flushes it, trying not to look at the brown-black mass of bodies swirling in the water.

The next couple of days are unproductive. He takes the dog on long walks, hoping to be inspired by nature, but all he sees are leaves changing colour. Soon, fall semester will start and he will be back at work. When colleagues ask about his retreat in the forest he'll have to grimace and say *It's not as easy as it looks*—or else *Wow, yeah, such a productive time*, shrivelling from the lie.

Each walk entails a lengthy cleaning process. There are muddy boots to deal with, but first the dog needs to be thoroughly brushed down before it can track dirt and dead leaves through the cabin. And it has acquired new ticks, of course. It seems a long time ago when they lived in the city, and the dog was a normal dog that didn't teem with its own vicious ecosystem.

His wife is late back from work, and he wonders what he would do if she simply failed to turn up. She has the car, and takes her cell to work with her. He plays the game of counting the tins in the cupboard, working out how long before he runs out of food. Would he starve to death, or learn to snare wild game? Perhaps the easiest thing would be to eat the dog.

When she finally shows up, grumbling about traffic, he senses she is resentful he hasn't started cooking. *But I might have been writing*, he thinks, and anyway he feels tired and out of sorts. By the next morning, this has developed into a full-blown cold. His wife stares in horrified disgust as he lies streaming and hacking. She cannot be ill; if she showed up at the studio with so much as a runny nose, her regulars would lose faith in the curative powers of yoga. She puts food and drink within reach of him and hurries out the door.

He spends the day drifting through a succession of unpleasant naps. They have not bathed the dog for more than a fortnight now, and it is too smelly to be allowed on the bed. Instead, it prowls around yapping, and the noise seeps into his head. He tries to feel victorious—a legitimate reason for inactivity—but his mind will not let him rest. What if today was the day he might have done something good? He begins forming the story he will tell others, of how illness derailed his writing streak.

He dreams that insects of all kinds are pressed against the windows of the cabin, the mass of bodies crushing the luckless ones in front so their carapaces burst against the glass. He dreams of swollen grey ticks all down his arm, like berries, gorging themselves on his blood, swelling to the size of grapes. When he wakes, there are raised red dots exactly where he dreamt they were. He flaps the sheets frantically, but there are no lurking ticks. *Psychosomatic*, his wife says, when he shows her the blistered arm. She spends the night on the couch, and when he still looks haggard the next day, urges him to see a doctor. *Just get me something from CVS, I'll be okay*, he says groggily, turning his head away so she won't nag. He certainly won't be able to do any writing in this state, but he has the confused notion that leaving the woods now would destroy the purity of his stay here.

It rains heavily that afternoon. He is woken by the

thrumming on the roof, an initial machine gun burst and then steady pounding, like a thousand typewriters going at once. He pulls a pillow over his head but it barely makes a difference. Giving up, he wanders into the living room, where the dog is cowering under an armchair. It is terrified of loud noises, and continues to tremble even after he picks it up and cradles it to his chest. Its eczema is getting worse.

Out of habit he begins combing the dog for ticks, but his heart isn't in it. He finds half a dozen and goes out onto the porch to flick them away. The rain is warm as it plops onto his arm, and impulsively he walks out into it, barefoot as he is, in his underpants. It is not the fat, tropical warmth of a monsoon, and all the more refreshing for it. The world becomes a room-temperature wall of water, an inverted bed of nails lightly massaging his scalp. He opens his arms to it. A baptism. This is the wettest he's ever been, wetter than a bath or deep-sea dive. He thinks of all the things that need washing away—the ticks, his illness, years of unproductivity and sloth and stultifying inertia. Some of the rainwater trickles into his mouth, but it is sour and gritty, not refreshing as he expected.

He leaves a trail of dirty footprints through the house. In the bathroom he dries himself carefully, hoping his wife won't ask about the sodden boxers in the sink. He is limp, the sudden gift of energy gone. Back in bed, he feels his skin fizz, and tries not to think about acid rain, or poisonous saps washing off the trees. The dog places its front paws on the footboard and whines. Too tired to argue, he lifts it, and it huddles against his body. He is getting used to its flaky, yeasty skin, the infections that ageing shih-tzus are prone to.

His wife is an hour late, then two. He finishes everything on the bedside table: saltine crackers, an apple, a juice carton. The dog eats the crumbs off the sheets then yaps and yaps until he gets up to feed it. Padding naked through the cabin, he notices the quiet—the rain has stopped. He tips dry food into a bowl and the dog attacks it. Most of its teeth are gone, and it has to grind each biscuit with its gums.

His wife does not come home that night. In the small hours he is still pressed against the window, hoping to see distant headlights. Many times in recent years he has wondered whether his uselessness and utter lack of accomplishment would begin to repel her. If she left him it would be like this, without warning. Her suitcase is here, of course, but she may have abandoned that too.

How many tins are in the cupboard? He makes a mental note to count again in the morning. Without the car, he is trapped—though starvation is not really an issue, the landlord will be along to reclaim his property in a couple of weeks. There are other lurid possibilities, which become more plausible as he tumbles through the night. The outbreak of war. Fast-spreading flu wiping out most of the Eastern seaboard. Or, more prosaic but just as terrifying, his wife dead in a five-car pile-up, no way for anyone to know he is stuck here.

Eventually, the dark fantasies blur into dreams, although he is later unsure at what point he falls asleep. Either the rain starts up again, or he has a nightmare that it does. A glowing rectangle beside his bed turns out to be his laptop screen. He opens the document containing his novel, but every word of it sickens him. There are only seven pages. He deletes the document and empties the trash can. It makes a sound like distant thunder. Then real lightning hits the roof and it springs a leak above his bed, only it is hundreds of ticks that trickle down right onto his chest. He swats them away, waking himself with the exertion. He must have scratched in his sleep, his torso is a mass of red welts. It is not yet dawn. He tries to get back to sleep as best he can, tangled in sweat-soaked sheets.

When he wakes properly, there is someone else in the house. A bear or burglar? His wife sticks her head round the door: *Oh good, the beast has risen*. She leaves a mug of coffee by the bed and begins tidying the room, explaining volubly about the storm throwing a tree trunk across the road, being stuck, spending the night on her brother's sofa.

I think I've been bitten, he starts to say, but before he can go on she has ripped the covers off and is looking dispassionately at his naked body. He knows her yoga instructor's eye is mechanically noting: middle-aged, sedentary, incipient beer-gut. There are now little red marks on his arms and legs. His face begins to itch and he wonders if they are there too.

You have chicken pox, she says, as if it is obvious. *I googled your symptoms. The kid the other day must have been infectious.* Reaching for her handbag, she pulls out calamine lotion in a bright pink tube, a gaping baby sprawled down one side. *The drugstore guy seemed to think it was for a child, I didn't correct him. Don't scratch, it might turn to shingles.* He hopes she will spread lotion on him, but she places the tube in his hand and strides away. Where is his laptop? He needs to check if he really has deleted his novel or if that was part of the dream—but what does it matter? A few scraps of imagination, paragraphs of drawn-out anguish. Even if it still exists, he will never look at it again.

He follows his wife into the kitchen, where she grudgingly butters some toast for him. *I suppose the dog hasn't had its breakfast?* Without waiting for an answer, she pours biscuits into the bowl. Every action seems to use a little more energy than is strictly necessary. She keeps up a monologue about how difficult it was to get time off work, the absurdity of a man pushing forty getting chicken pox, and then the kicker, *You're not even a real writer*, like Dan Brown. *No one's heard of you.*

There is nothing he can say to that, and anyway his whole body is heavy with a dull pain, his head stuffed solid. He rests it on the table until he can get enough strength together to drag himself back to bed. Then he hears his wife say, with more tenderness than he has heard from her in a decade,

You're not doing great, are you? Poor baby, it hasn't been easy for you. Such caresses in her voice. Despite himself, a flicker of hope rises in his chest, a needle-thin crack of light. He looks up, ready to say something, then realises she was speaking to the dog.

Schwellenangst

SHE CAN MAKE out the words in the fading sunlight: "The only good system is a sound system." The long, concrete façade is at least a kilometre long, and the expanse has clearly defeated its vandals, who have marred it only in patches. She has walked past several stretches still pristine grey, damaged only by the salt air and bird droppings. Some of the windows are broken—often with chairs or bottles protruding through the glass—some covered in wooden boards, and a rare few still intact.

Joy pulls out her phone and takes a photo of the English sentence. It will make a good cover for her Facebook page. Most of the graffiti is in German, but language here is no badge of authenticity. Everyone she has met seems eager to parade their English before her, once they work out she speaks it more or less at native level. Even the older residents, the ones whose second language at school was Russian, pepper their dialogue with trendy words. "Auf meinem To-do List stehen drei Urgent Emails."

Her own German is fairly rusty, but good enough to cope with ordinary conversation. She isn't too bothered about getting things like gender right. It makes no sense, anyway, that "sea" is feminine but "ocean" neutral. She tries both out, looking at the glittering water just visible through a screen of pine trees. "Das Meer. Die Ostsee." It is the Baltic, on the Northern German coast. From a high enough place, on a clear day, they say you can see Sweden.

She has been walking for forty-five minutes now, and there is no sign the building will surprise her. Its uniformity is its strength, what gives it the sheer brute force of a monolithic bulwark against—what? The locals, when they refer to it at all, call it the Hitler Building. On the way over, when they stopped for lunch, the fat woman who ran the café tried to talk them out of staying there. "Go to Binz instead," she insisted. "Nicer there. Not so much history."

Joy tried to explain that history was exactly what they were after, why the school was sending twenty-three of its brightest A-Level candidates at hugely subsidised prices on a journey away from anything normal teenagers might find exciting. No shopping or nightclubs. The Head of Department having decided that the way to truly understand a language is to know the past of its speakers, they have gone in search of artefacts.

And now, Prora. They arrived that afternoon and have seen the museum, but the real exploration will take place tomorrow. Her solo walk around is ostensibly so she can identify potential problems in their route, but really so she can experience the building without the distraction of two dozen well-meaning but unbiddable young people. The daytrippers have long gone, and she has the narrow footpath to herself.

Even with the wind, she can hear vague throbbing that resolves into a bass line as she nears the row of windows with light behind them. Not the steady glow of normal lamps, but flickers and flashes. Torches? Then she gets closer and it is obvious. As she watches, a tallish red-haired man steps from a window, finding his footing on the ledge, lighting a cigarette. They eye each other. She shouts up, "Entschuldigung, ist hier einen Rave?" Hoping the German word is the same as in English. They so often are.

He shrugs. "Call it what you like." His English is excellent, with only a trace of accent. "Come up, come in, if you like. Why not?"

There are many reasons why not, but she finds herself testing the first step of the ladder, gripping a rung, easing herself up. The man waits, and offers her the hand which isn't holding his cigarette. "Peter," he says into her ear.

"Joy," she offers in return. Now that she is up here, she can feel the music like a physical force, right through the thick walls and empty windows. He leads her through one of them into the room, still smoking, and she has the impression of hotel room furniture tortured by birds and rainwater, the passage of time, spiderwebs layered thickly over the ceiling.

It's hard to be sure how big the space is, it's lit only by candles and a couple of incongruous anglepoise desk-lamps.

Peter hands her a beer. "Should I—?" She isn't sure how to complete the question, but he shrugs again, in a comfortable way that suggests he does this a lot, popping the bottle open by slamming it against a table edge. She accepts it carefully, wiping the rim before putting her lips to it. "Vielen Dank."

"You like this?" says Peter loudly, his hair gleaming like copper in the hazy light, and she nods. "My husband would be shocked if he knew I was in a place like this," she says, enunciating carefully over the noise, wishing she remembered how to do the conditional tense in German. He smiles like a wolf to show he understands, his eyes drooping knowingly as if to say, *You didn't need to do that, in you I have no interest.*

There are about twenty bodies in the space, mostly older than she'd have expected—some even in their thirties. They are dancing in a listless, bobbing kind of way, but then the music is some kind of European house, not really what she'd have expected, not all that different to a normal nightclub anywhere. Perhaps the location is the only subversive thing about this gathering. While stepping over the window sill, she'd made a mental note to refuse any drugs she was offered, but this now seems an unlikely contingency.

Peter is waving at a girl, who walks over to them. "My twin sister, Sigrid," he says into her ear. She has the same shade of hair, also matted and unruly. Joy smiles uncertainly and she responds by leaning forward for an air kiss, which ends awkwardly as Joy can never decipher whether one or both cheeks are called for. "Not very rock and roll," says Sigrid cheerfully, and drags them both onto the dance floor.

It's been a while since Joy has danced. She can't blame her marriage for this, or even turning thirty—she just fell out of the habit. It's not something she's particularly missed, but now that she's here again, it's surprisingly easy to fall back into the rhythm of it, looking at the other people in the group now and again, holding your beer so it doesn't spill, remembering to move your legs and not just your arms and head. Peter and Sigrid are better at this, long-limbed and dextrous.

After twelve songs or so, Joy begins to feel bored, and this too is something she remembers from her clubbing days. Even when the melodies vary, all dancing ever seems to be is reaching for the beat and moving more or less in time to it. These are too samey to interest her, all cool detached topnotes with electronic riffs, as if a robot somewhere were assembling them out of parts. She looks at her watch, thinking she'll go if it's been more than an hour, but it's too dark to see. She can keep going. It's not dull exactly, but she wouldn't be heartbroken to leave.

Around the third time she has this thought, when her beer is dangling emptily and she is wondering if it's possible to get another one, Peter nods at the window and Sigrid

smiles, and then all three of them are scampering down the
ladder like children and in the damp night air. "Enough,"
says Sigrid, as if instructing an apprentice. "The art of parties
is knowing when to leave."

"Who organises this?" says Joy, eliciting another shrug
from Peter. "Someone. Some people. They come here from
the town. There is not much happening here on Rügen, I
think. They party and they leave. We heard about this from
a friend. We came to look."

"Where in Germany do you come from?"

"Where in Germany?" Peter mimics. "Stockholm. There
in Germany. Did you think we sound German?"

Joy is about to apologise, though she isn't sure for what,
when they laugh and instead she asks, "How long have you
been here?"

"On the island?" Peter shrugs. "We arrived yesterday. It's
easy for us to get here, Sweden is just over there." He gestures
vaguely towards the trees, to the dappled water beyond.

"Are you just here for the party?"

"What else?"

Joy starts to explain about her school sending her, but the
alcohol seems to have thickened her tongue and the wind
keeps snatching her voice away, and it takes a while. By now
they have wandered far enough that the music is no longer
audible. Peter produces three tins of beer from a pocket of
his cargo pants and doles them out. She takes one. Why not?

"But then where are your students?" Sigrid wants to know.

"There are three other teachers. We've agreed to take turns having the night off."

"Are they well-behaved?"

"The teachers? Oh, we all are, the students too. Singaporeans are famous for being well-behaved."

"Oh, you are from Singapore." Joy smiles warily, ready for the next question, which is usually something about chewing gum or how small the country is. Instead, Peter says thoughtfully, his head as if to study her from a different angle, "But you are not, Chinese? Sorry, I do not—"

"Eurasian," says Joy. "There are a lot of races in Singapore."

"What means Eurasian?"

She shrugs. "A mixture. A bit of Europe, a bit of Asia." This is an over-simplification, but it seems to satisfy them. "I suppose you don't have that where you are?"

"No," says Sigrid, deadpan. "Everyone looks the same in Sweden. We can only tell each other apart by hair colour."

They have reached a sandy, shallow slope, dotted with fir trees and swept by the unseen ocean. It is tempting to suggest a dip in the dark, but they were warned at the youth hostel about dangerous currents, and the water is probably cold. Already, the evening is falling into more orderly lines, and Joy instinctively knows that the single aberration of the not-quite-rave is all she has an appetite for. As they find a place to sit, she is aware of her sensible shoes, her glasses, her utter lack of what Sigrid would call "rock and roll". But that is fine. She will have a nice chat with her new friends, and then head to bed.

"You are staying nearby?"

"In the Jugendherberge." She gargles her r's a little, which she has learnt makes her sound like a more proficient speaker.

"Oh." Sigrid wrinkles her nose. "We passed by earlier. All neat, ping pong table and barbecue pit outside? I don't know why people stay in this place."

"It's convenient. You come here to party."

"That is different. The building is empty, ruined, we don't pretend it's fine, we see it and we dance. But that side— painted white, pretending it's so nice and perfect, no."

Joy takes a pull from her beer, not sure if she can formulate a coherent response.

"Do you know the history of this?" says Peter.

"Of course. We're here to study the history. To experience the place."

"My grandmother wanted to stay here," says Sigrid unexpectedly. "I read her old diaries, when she died. She talked about Prora like it was paradise, from the pictures she saw. She said how great the Führer was, to build this. Cheap holidays for workers."

"Kraft durch Freude," says Joy.

"Freedom through happiness, yes. Bread and circuses."

"Your grandmother?"

"She was German. So were my parents. They came to Sweden."

"And now you're staying here instead."

"We thought we would see if there is any furniture left in the bedrooms," says Peter. "But now I think we will sleep here. Siggy? Here it is nice."

"If it does not rain." Sigrid rests her head on Peter's bony knee, her hair thrown back so it fans over his lap. He leans forward, his skinny back arching, and kisses her hard on the mouth. She raises herself on her elbows. When they are done, Peter winks at Joy. "She is not really my twin."

"Did you say that?" Sigrid tilts her head back. "He does that sometimes. It is maybe amusing because we look quite similar."

"You believed?" Peter waggles his ring finger at her. "Wife, not sister."

"Congratulations" is all Joy can think to say.

"See how it turns out before you congratulate."

Sigrid smacks him across the shoulder. "What is Singapore like, Joy?"

"Smaller than Rügen. Clean. I don't know."

"Do you have anything like this?"

"A five-kilometre-long concrete hotel built by Hitler? No."

"Then no wonder you would come here to see it."

Joy checks her phone. No messages or missed calls—

everything must be all right. She is surprised by the time, later than she thought. They students will be asleep by now, or at least in bed. They have an early start in the morning, a visit to the museum and then a guided tour of those parts of the ruins it is safe to walk in. The ballroom, the many swimming pools, the dining hall designed to serve meals for twenty thousand in shifts. A sandwich lunch, provided by the youth hostel, and then back on the coach for their next destination. More history.

This is meant to be the most exciting part of her job, educational travel, but so far it has been largely pedestrian. The only requirement is they return with the same number of students they left with. So it's just this evening—and she has a flash of how odd this is, like a movie, that she is here with these people. The Swedes are completely relaxed, as if they are used to the loose ebb and flow of people in the world. They enjoy her company—they must or they wouldn't still be here—but she knows that at the end of the evening they will not be swapping e-mail addresses or promising to add each other on Facebook.

"Where will you go after this?" says Peter, combing Sigrid's long hair with his fingers.

"We'll head along the coast for a bit—to see the towers, the watchtowers—"

"Grenzturm."

"Is that them? The ones they used to look out for people trying to escape."

"Yes, Grenzturm. For anyone swimming to the West. They used to shine searchlights level with the water to spot them more easily. Still, people tried, and got shot. My aunt froze to death. She thought it would be easier in the winter."

Sigrid volunteers this so matter-of-factly that Joy takes a moment to be sure she has heard it. "Your family was here?"

"My aunt married someone from here. My mother was in Berlin."

"Which side?"

"East, of course. We were all in the East. She could see the wall from her bedroom window, when she was a girl. It was so close. But of course, not close enough to— There was a viewing platform on the other side. People from the West would stand there, waving over the wall, or just looking. Holding up placards like 'Down with Communism' or 'We are solidarity with you'. My mother waved back sometimes. Then one day, she was looking, and you know, she saw—"

"She saw herself, a doppelgänger in the West," says Peter, in his ghost-story voice.

Sigrid smacks him. "No. You are a dick. She saw her friend, Beata. Her best friend from school."

"How did she get across?"

"She didn't know. Of course, some people crossed, and you wouldn't tell your friends before you went. Beata waved, but maybe not at her. She never saw her again. Later, they came and covered all the windows with bricks."

"We're going to Berlin, with the students. Leipzig, then Berlin."

"Bernauerstrasse, my mother's street. You should visit. There is still a platform there, and they have kept a part of the wall. For souvenir."

"Did she ever get out?"

"No, she didn't try." Sigrid's beautiful face is unreadable. Peter has tuned out, not unsympathetically, but Joy can tell he has heard this story before, more than once. "We left like everyone else, when the wall fell."

"1990."

"It's funny, we heard it was happening, but I was going to school like normal and my mother had a cold so she said we should all sleep early that night. My father didn't really care about the news, he said nothing would ever change, just one wall won't make a difference. But the next day our neighbour said, 'What are you doing, you are missing the biggest event of your life.' So we drove there, not very far, and then there were so many people we couldn't move, so we got out and walked. There was a big smash in the concrete, nothing like we've ever seen, all the way through the two walls, outer and in. We went through and the people on the other side were like us, but not so, how do you call, grey? A woman put her hand on my cheek and gave me sweets."

"And then you were in the West."

"For a few hours, yes, then we went back. I had to do my

homework and my mother wanted to cook dinner. We went across again on the weekend; there were fewer people then and more of the wall was missing. It was more normal to walk across, and no one welcomed us like before. I asked my mother where the people with the sweets were. She laughed and said life in the West would not always be so much fun. A few weeks later we moved to Sweden."

"Why Sweden?"

"Why not? It was the West. She hadn't seen anything of the West. Maybe she remembered her sister, trying to swim across to Sweden. Not so far, but far enough."

There is a silence, and then Peter says, gently, "She came to Sweden so she could meet me." It sounds almost like a joke, but there is a stillness in his voice that was not there before. He lowers himself onto his elbows so Sigrid can fit her body against his, sliding together as if their curves and grooves were made to match.

"And now," says Sigrid, "I am Swedish."

"But you came back."

"I wanted to see."

"You have walls in your country too? Great Wall," says Peter.

"Singapore isn't part of China," says Joy, without rancour. "And the Great Wall was to keep people out, not in."

"Most walls do both," says Sigrid.

They talk about nothing much, what will happen next.

The Swedes have no plan, they will hitchhike off Rügen, and see where they end up next, or maybe they will take a ferry to Norway. They have a bit of money saved up, and travel is cheap when it is summer and you will spend most of your nights sleeping in the open.

And behind them, still visible in the moonlight, is the great concrete slab of Prora. Really, they are between two walls, that and the screen of trees shielding them from the full force of the sea winds. Joy is looking forward to seeing what remains of the Berlin wall—"Mauer", she remembers, not "Wand" like an interior wall. The few stretches they have allowed to stay, and the line that marks the rest. There are fewer walls where she comes from, but she remembers, as a child, asking her parents about the one around their condominium. *So the bad people can't see what we have*, she was told. *Or they might come and rob us.*

This feels like the end of the night, the wind softening its tone, now like a lullaby, like the last slow song before the nightclub turns its lights on. How unlikely that she should be here, thousands of miles from the place she was born. No walls for her. She carefully brushes sand off her blouse and thinks, *I should get back*, but stays for just a moment longer, enjoying the sounds and sap-smells of the night.

Peter and Sigrid are quiet now, but there isn't enough light to tell if they are asleep. She doesn't want to speak, it would spoil something, whatever is circling in the air around them. Joy collects long German words; she enjoys how they are concertinaed together from shorter ones, how there is always one for the specific sensation of each moment. Right now, it would be Waldeinsamkeit, the feeling of being alone in the woods. Not necessarily a literal forest, though there are enough trees within easy reach. As she shuts her eyes, she lists compound words. Schadenfreude, of course. Verschlimmbesserung, a so-called improvement that actually makes things worse. Schwellenangst, the fear of crossing thresholds, or boundaries.

Joy dreams of being in a maze, of running through a limitless number of turnings and crossroads, all of which might lead to more choices, or to a dead end. And on either side of her are walls too high and smooth to climb, so tall she can only dimly see the sky above her, and a glimmer of the moon. It feels like just the other side of the walls are all the people she has lost, not visible but still present. Those who died, those who drifted away. The missing teacher is there too, the one who taught at her school and then just disappeared last March holidays. Where did she go? There is no one in sight, just her, just the path ahead. Kraft durch Freude, she tells herself. Strength through Joy.

She wakes up with a niggle of disquiet in her mind, a persistent crick in her neck, but most of all a warmth and well-being that radiates through every cell in her body. The sun is already up, an intense point low in the swimming-pool sky, bright in a different way to Singapore, more scorching than roasting. It's going to be a hot day. A moment of panic as she looks at her watch, but it is not yet seven; she has plenty of time to walk back, shower, and present herself at breakfast as if none of this has happened. She won't tell anyone, not even her husband—not for any reason, he wouldn't mind, and not to erase it either, but just because.

The Swedes are still asleep beside her, their skin even paler against the tangle of red hair by daylight. She looks at them a moment, decides against taking a picture, and waves goodbye although they cannot see her. She should go. If any of the students are awake already—well, she'll have to pretend she was out on a morning stroll.

It is not far to the hostel, and she allows herself to meander through the trees. Prora is to her right, and although she looks hard for clues, she cannot work out which set of windows the party was in. Even with the graffiti as a marker, the surface is too uniform. And to her left is the Baltic Sea, flexing its surface with strong, regular waves. The green-black water reaches all the way to the horizon, and she imagines that she can just see, in the distance, other lands.

Sophia's Aunt

WHEN DOCTOR'S WORDS confound Sophia's patchy Mandarin, she says *Pardon?* but he just grows unhelpfully louder. Finally she says *Wait, wait* and calls her aunt. As the phone rings, she imagines the aunt's ungainly progress through the camphorous apartment, catching her knee on the rosewood armchair, swearing in pungent bursts.

A click and muffled thud as the aunt pulls at the cord and demands, breathlessly, *Yes?*

I don't know what Doctor wants. Can you ask him? Sophia has learnt that her aunt regards hellos and how-are-yous as wasted words, wasted time. She hands the phone to Doctor and leans her head against the smeary window as they have a quacking conversation. From four stories up, the view is bleak—gunmetal grey and churning dust. Yet whenever she mentions the pollution to a local, the reply is always the same: *You should have seen it before the Olympics; it was a luxury to see the sky then.*

A finger jabs her impatiently. It is Doctor, thrusting the phone back at her. The aunt says, *He wanted to know about the*—and then a jumble of sounds. *I don't*— Sophia begins, and the aunt sighs. *Artificial heart*, she says in English. *Mechanical.*

We didn't want that, protests Sophia. *Gu Ma, can you tell him*— she calls the woman Gu Ma, "Aunt", even though she is Sophia's father's cousin, not his sister, from the branch of the family that stayed in China instead of coming to Singapore more than half a century ago.

Sophia passes the phone back to Doctor and they squawk away again. Both have Beijing accents, their voices arch and slurred. Her head aches. The noise is amplified by the narrow corridor, which smells not of antiseptic, as a hospital should, but of concrete and radiator dust. Doctor slots the phone into her hand as if she were a wall socket and marches away. She lifts it to her ear, but the aunt has already hung up.

She retrieves her bags from the nurses' station and continues on to Nicholas's ward. At visiting hours, families leave their doors open so the building feels like a many-storeyed village, children shuffling in corners and noisy wives telling husbands the latest gossip. She wanted Nicholas to go to a private clinic but the aunt vetoed that—the care wouldn't be as good. *Korean doctors*, she sniffed. *Japanese nurses.*

They have at least insisted on a private ward. It is important that Nicholas has restful surroundings before his operation, and he can always earn the money to pay for this after his recovery. She turns a corner and the grinding noises of the lifts fade. The doors are farther apart here. They are the only foreigners in this section, though if she does not speak she can pass for a local.

Nicholas is watching television when she comes in, although he can't understand a word of Chinese. He claims to follow the sense, but she thinks he just wants a voice in the room. She has left him a small stack of index cards on which her aunt has written "Bring water" or "Turn down heating". A chaste kiss, as always, then she begins pulling containers from her bags. Over Sophia's protests, the aunt insisted on doing the cooking. *Your cooking is the reason he's sick*, she retorted, and there was enough truth in that to silence Sophia. She still remembers the consultant, after his first collapse, talking about hypertension, the silent killer; blaming stress as well as too much fat and salt—and her guilty recollection of all those steaks fried in butter, all that French patisserie.

The hospital does not provide food, which had surprised Sophia, but then she is not sure she would have trusted anything they served. She pushes the folding table out across Nicholas's bed, and places bowls and plastic containers within easy reach. He will not eat all of this, the variety is intended only to stimulate his appetite. She sets out double-boiled soup—just a little, they are supposed to be restricting fluid intake—stewed pork, steamed fish, fluffy white rice. He brings a shaky spoonful to his mouth.

Sophia goes to the market every morning with the aunt,

paying pennies for an array of meats, fish lifted live from a basin and splayed open in front of them, making sure everything is fresh and untainted. She has heard terrible stories about processed foods. One is playing out on the news at the moment: a milk powder scandal, babies dying from formula adulterated with melamine. She shudders, imagining sniffing at a bottle—*Something's off. A bit too chalky? No, I'm sure it's fine…*

When Nicholas has had enough, the food goes back into the tote bags it arrived in, boxes slotting neatly together, cutlery wrapped in a paper towel. She pours him some tea from a thermos and blows to cool it before touching it to his lips. In the first days, she felt the need to keep up a stream of chat, filling the dead air. Now she sees that her presence is enough. She reads him an article from *The Economist*—something about Elizabeth Warren, which he snorts at, a glimpse of his old self.

The nurses come as usual, day shift handing over to night. Both are young, alike enough to be sisters. They smile and jabber rapidly over his chart. Sophia is sure they linger in the doorway longer than is strictly necessary, as if still taken with the novelty of having a white man on their floor. Finally, she thanks them pointedly and they go.

They did more tests today, says Nicholas, shrugging as if to forestall her next question. *Who knows what for?* They took some blood, labelled it, and packed the vials neatly into a plastic box that whizzed off on a trolley. So much of him, circulating in unknown parts of the hospital.

Sophia nods, then remembers. *The doctor said something about a mechanical heart. I got Gu Ma to say you'd never had one—though I'm not sure if he was asking that, or if you wanted one.* This was an option they'd been offered in Singapore, when it became clear that Nicholas did not meet the criteria to get on the transplant waiting list. It seemed plausible at first. What is the heart except a pump, what does it do that a machine cannot? But this would only ever be a temporary measure, and he didn't want to live a patchwork life, buying one year at a time, never knowing how much longer—

They already have this information, he says. *They keep asking me the same questions. I hope nothing's—*

Gu Ma says nothing will go wrong. You're a textbook case. The aunt works with liver, but knows someone in the heart work-unit and managed to get Nicholas admitted that way. *As long as you're able to pay, she said. They'll do a good job for you.*

They slip into another silence. She straightens his bedspread, which is far too short for him; his feet stick out at the end. His toenails need cutting, but she has not brought clippers. The sunlight has almost gone by the time she puts on the light, which shows up stained linoleum, grimy salmon-pink walls. She has never actually seen a cockroach in the building, but suspects they lurk just out of sight.

When Nicholas collapsed, her first thought was that this must be one of his opaque practical jokes, embarrassing her in the middle of IKEA. She stood helpless, cross, until people came running. A store assistant started CPR. Understanding only arrived with the ambulance. She sat in the back, thinking, *But this doesn't happen to people like us*.

How long ago was that? Months. Weeks. She finds it hard to pin time down, and in the eternal summer of Singapore there are no natural breaks of season to mark its passing, only school holidays for those so afflicted. She sometimes passes on news of the outside world—a new Goldman Sachs scandal, some faraway natural disaster—which he contrives to seem interested in, but really the world has shrunk to the two of them, just these walls, just the stubborn passages inside his heart which will not function as they should.

We're so lucky Gu Ma brought us here, she says ritualistically, for maybe the tenth time, unsure whether she is trying to arouse gratitude in herself, or merely appear grateful so the universe will not take even this chance away from them. *Yes*, says Nicholas. *Very lucky*. They could never, on their own, have negotiated their way into this hospital, not without the aunt to speak to certain people, to scribble her way through swathes of paperwork with the élan of someone who's lived her life within a low-tech bureaucracy.

They play a word-hunt game on her iPad and Nicholas cheats flagrantly, which she pretends not to notice. It is a relief when Nurse comes to tell her to please leave, come again tomorrow. Sophia kisses her husband's dry lips and joins the families clustering in the hallways, laughing and shouting at children to stop running. Her insides are heavy, as if the grey outside sky has taken up residence in her. She is somehow unable to fit into the rhythm of the people around her, and keeps getting bumped into.

Her phone rings as she reaches the car park. She knows it will be the aunt, and breathes in-out rapidly three times before pressing "answer". *Gu Ma?*

Finished? Can't pick you up today. Meeting. The aunt has a lot of meetings. Sophia has not been able to decipher what these might be—something to do with work, or the Party? She does not want to know.

That's fine, she says. *I'll take a taxi*. She remembers to use the proper Mandarin word, "jichengche", not the Singaporean "deshi"—a bastardisation of the English.

Don't tell the driver where you're from.

Sophia sighs. *Don't worry. I'll just say I'm from the South.* The aunt is certain that all Beijing taxi drivers, being rogues, will overcharge her mercilessly if they find out she is foreign.

I don't know what time I'll be back. Don't wait for me to eat.

Yes. Sophia hesitates, but the words bubble up. *Gu Ma, will he be all right?*

The aunt sniffs. *Don't worry for nothing. Old Cheng will do a good job. He's done so many hearts over the years—for him, it's just like putting a new battery into your alarm clock.* Old Cheng is the former colleague. Sophia isn't very sure about how they are connected. Camp-mates during re-education? Something like that.

Thank you, says Sophia to the click of the aunt hanging up.

The sky is inky blue as she walks round to the front of the building, the roadside trees are sharp silhouettes. She thinks of the Chinese word "qing", which means something between black and green, the exact colour of a tree at dusk.

That was a good phone call, she considers. Talking to the aunt is an obstacle course, especially with her limited Mandarin. She counts a conversation successful if it passes without real awkwardness on either side. It doesn't help that she barely knows the aunt—their families were only able to get back in touch after China opened its borders in the eighties. She has a childhood memory of a loud-voiced woman visiting once, her clothes plain and washed thin, smelling of unaired rooms. She is in her sixties now, a squat figure with formidable powers of persuasion.

It can't have been easy being a female doctor, and perhaps this is why the aunt never married. Sophia knows she should show an interest, but can't find the energy to ask these questions—to find out some of what the last fifty years have been like. And there are always more pressing things to discuss: Nicholas's food, Nicholas's medicine. She remembers her father once saying something about high-powered friends, about how she could have risen higher if not for political factions—but this is all part of the wall of unknowing that now surrounds Sophia: China, the aunt's past, Nicholas's illness. Each overwhelming, too large to contemplate or unpick.

Outside the hospital is a sculpture on a tall pedestal. High overhead, two bronze hands, each the size of a man's head, clasp each other, the lower hand clearly being pulled out of some danger. The upper hand is fringed with the edge of a sleeve, on which it is just possible to make out the emblem of a five-pointed star, heraldic leaves below it.

Her own hands clasped for warmth, Sophia stands by the road. Even though winter is supposed to be on its way out. the air is chilly. She shivers as she checks that she still has all her bags. A man is selling roasted chestnuts nearby, his brazier exuding charred, smoky fumes. *If only I could be saved*, she thinks, stretching her arm out into the road to stop a taxi.

■ ■ ■

At two in the morning, the concrete walls begin to sweat. They must turn off the heating at night for the building to chill so rapidly. This is Nicholas's worst time of night, when he gives up trying to force himself into sleep. Perhaps tonight it is better this way, rather than sleeping through what could be his last hours of life.

He tries to divert his mind, but now it slips into well-trammelled lines. If he dies on the table—or if he lives, but is no better off than before—or if it works, and he is magically back the way he was before, strong and whole, and they can go home. None of these possibilities feel real to him, and there seems to be no reason why he shouldn't be here forever, in this dank bunker of a room, listening to the coughs seeping in from adjacent wards.

Most of all, it seems inconceivable that a stranger's heart will beat inside his chest. He has spent the day visualising the heart of each person around him, doctors, cleaners, even Sophia—stripping away the layers, skin and fat and muscle, laying bare the dark red core, pistons pumping or sluicing in their grooves. He imagines giant scalpels neatly filching one swollen muscle, replacing it with another.

It has been a year of strangeness. The blank disbelief on Sophia's face as they stretchered him away. All the way to the hospital, Sophia squeezed his hand. When he told her this, she said it was impossible, he didn't recover consciousness until later that afternoon. Now he keeps his recollections to himself.

His vocabulary has expanded over this year. He has learnt the precise medical terms for each of his symptoms—the heaviness keeping him awake is pulmonary oedema, his weak heart no longer able to pump the fluid from his lungs. He knows the difference between aortic and ventricular aneurysms. Some of this comes from doctors, but also hearsay, piles of medical journals, and most of all the Internet. The last few days have been a release, no Wi-Fi at the hospital, the firewall preventing Sophia even reading out good wishes on Facebook: the deadening parade of friends who feel they ought to say something.

He makes a list in his head of people who might miss him when he is gone. He has no family to speak of. Sophia, of course—but for how long? And friends—but again, he can think of only a couple he would want in the room right now. Can he remember the names of all thirty-four MBA classmates, all twenty-seven people from his college choir? How many of them will remember him?

But this is morbid. He reaches for his bedside water bottle before remembering that it's been taken away, the nurses placing their hands firmly across their mouths in a gesture of abstinence. He remembers an episode from his childhood: their family cat wasn't supposed to eat anything before the spaying, but it jumped up on the breakfast table and snatched a scrap of food. They took it to the vet anyway, and it died under anaesthetic, choking to death on regurgitated ham.

If Sophia were here—and now he feels resentful that she is not. She would have stayed, but he sent her away. He couldn't allow it. He'd be fine, he was a big boy. All the things he felt he was expected to say. And so she went off to spend another night on the aunt's creaky sleeper-sofa, probably little more comfortable than one of the plastic hospital chairs, or indeed his current bed. He feels that she might have offered one more time.

And once again his mind fills with Sophia. He will never get to sleep at this rate. If she were here, if she were to attain one of her rare periods of calm—when she is still, her outline no longer flickering, her voice suddenly gentle. If she would just pull her fingers through his hair, just once, knead the precise spot on his neck that makes all the tension leave his body. Tears prickle at his eyes and he is horrified. To be sniffling like a schoolboy when he will see her tomorrow!

He imagines himself whole again. Perhaps a year, Doctor said—at least according to Sophia's translation, which he mistrusts. He suspects her of eliding inconvenient statements, or glossing over words she does not understand. She has never been particularly good at Mandarin. At her school, she once told him, it was an article of pride to speak it badly, to be ultra-fluent in English instead—and he has noticed her anxious, furrowed concentration whenever Doctor speaks.

Nicholas is still a young man with almost all his hair, but must acknowledge his outline is not as firm as it once was. He runs his hands over his belly, comfortably flat now he is lying down, and wonders if this degradation is the result of a year of enforced indolence—no gym, no five-a-side—or the inevitable decline of a man in his middle thirties, the first supports giving way before the entire edifice collapses. *When*

I am strong again, he promises, *I will start jogging.*

The wall clock opposite the bed is barely visible. He squints through the gloom, trying to distinguish the minute hand from shadow. Is the short hand before or after three? He doesn't want to turn on the light and bring himself to full wakefulness. At least in the dark he can glide along the surface of consciousness. Several times now he has felt a shift, as if he'd fallen into a stretch of light sleep, or at least had his mind empty momentarily.

This is his eighth night in Beijing, a city he has visited many times before, but never really seen. His memories are mostly of the insides of buildings—meeting rooms, cocktail bars. A world of work that once seemed barely tolerable, a laughable exercise in moneymaking until real success found him. Now he finds he cannot wait to get back to it. To knot his tie, step into polished shoes, allow the numbers to run through his brain, familiar as slipping into a warm bath.

He has been out with Sophia only once in Beijing, on a day when the low winter sunlight seemed too enticing to ignore. They took a taxi to one of the large parks, full of humanity even on such a cold day. *Huai Hai Gong Yuan*, Sophia read doubtfully off the sign at the entrance. *"Hai" is "sea", maybe that's the lake?* They had to pay to go in. His skin was grey in full daylight, actually grey.

The afternoon was a disaster. Sophia veered between brittle cheerfulness and snapping at him for making fun of a woman's hair. *She probably doesn't speak English*, he protested, but she was already marching stiffly ahead. He was in hospital slippers, which forced him to shuffle like an old man. Next time, he resolved, he would make an effort and put on lace-up shoes. Only Sophia never offered to take him out again.

The walls feel impenetrable, claustrophobic. He has never felt so constrained as now. Both alone and with Sophia, he has always been able to simply board a plane to take him where he needed to be. The first sealed door wasn't actually the illness, it was being told by the hospital in Singapore that he was considered a poor candidate for a transplant; it was learning from a harassed-sounding woman in a Newcastle call-centre that, having lived outside the UK for so long, he is no longer eligible for NHS treatment. The cost of a private operation made his eyes widen. Why hadn't they saved more? Or bothered taking out insurance?

He remembers his watch and rummages in the drawer for it. It is designed for diving and lights up at the touch of a button. A little after four o'clock. He must surely have slept a little, even if he wasn't aware of it. He can't have been up all these hours, chasing thoughts around his head. Even now the lines in his head will not stay orderly, they bend and twist around each other. This is wrong. He isn't supposed to be agitated. Even though he hasn't smoked since university, he desperately wants a cigarette now.

It is so still now, the quietest hour of the night. He thinks he can hear his own heart beating. Normal, no stutter, no slowing down, just a regular thud. What will they do with it? A bin full of medical waste somewhere, and— his imagination fails him. Presumably the risk of contamination rules out landfill, so the incinerator? All those scraps of bodies, fat melting, small hairs catching fire, igniting skin, and in the middle of that his heart, deep red, trailing white slime.

He feels a knot inside him dissolve, as if it is made of sugar, and he is calm. A deep stillness, the city letting out its breath, a pause before it draws the next. What else can he do? For the first time in weeks, there is no pain between his shoulder blades. This may be the resignation of a condemned man approaching the scaffold, but there is strength in it too. *You can do nothing further to me*, he thinks. *After the trapdoor opens, gravity takes over.*

A bubble of noise just outside his door: creaking, rattling wheels and rough voices. He is routinely woken just before dawn by the cleaners, who will not enter his room till much later but announce their presence, distributing cleaning supplies at regular intervals along the corridor like dogs peeing to mark their territory. They chatter constantly, louder than the nurses, louder than can possibly be necessary with no competing sounds. Sophia may be hesitant when she speaks Mandarin, but at least her tone is pleasantly modulated, obviously educated.

He closes his eyes for a moment, and when he opens them again the corridor is silent and sunlight has appeared on the wall. Actual sunlight, the yellow of a broken egg, finger-streaked through the Venetian blinds, not the pearly grey light he wakes up to most mornings. Something unhooks inside him—excitement from a past life, rustling grass that seems to say: spring is on its way. He has lived in Singapore too long, absorbed too much of its constant tropical sun. Now he remembers the pleasure of seasons, the sudden lightness of an afternoon without a coat.

Nicholas feels his anger slip away. It isn't fair that his parents are dead, that he is alone in this box of a room with its patchy walls, his own body betraying him. But he lets this drift away, and soon it is beyond his field of vision. Sophia's indifference, her maddening aunt, the head-drilling voices of the cleaning staff—one after another they float into darkness. He has always been the kind of man who builds up quiet rage over weeks before releasing it in tight, barely courteous words. Not now. He inches a toe forward until it just touches the pool of sun, convinced he feels a gradual warmth blossom over his body.

By the time the nurse comes in—without knocking, as usual—he is able to watch her completely placidly, not tensing as footsteps approach the door. She seems unnerved by his attempt at a smile. There are a few things she must do—take his temperature, check his chart—and she goes through them studiously, as if he is a puzzle that requires great attention to solve.

Perhaps it is the sleepless night, but the next hour passes in a fog. He is wheeled down a corridor, his chest shaved, or perhaps the other way round. So many lights. They flare above his head, making squiggles across his retina. Each time he opens his eyes, his surroundings have shifted. Everyone is speaking, sometimes all at once, but probably not to him. Sophia flickers past him, though later he can't remember if his eyes were open or shut when he saw her. They inject various liquids into him. He feels oddly little pain, and then none at all.

■ ■ ■

Soon you will be going home, says the aunt. Sophia jumps, having been staring out of the car window. The aunt repeats herself.

Maybe, says Sophia. *Probably. It depends what the doctor says.*

I've enjoyed having you here. The aunt is unusually abstracted today, not shouting at any other drivers even though they have been stuck in traffic for forty minutes now, and motorcycles keep veering perilously close, threatening to snap off her wing mirror.

We'll visit again. There is more that Sophia wants to add to this—how grateful she is, how sorry that she doesn't know her aunt better—but the right words fail to come together in her mind. There must be polite formulae for these situations. *I should have watched more TV*, she thinks. How many soap opera scenes there must be of awkward car journeys, family members reaching tentatively towards each other—and the stock phrases they use, the last refuge of the lazy screenwriter. If only she knew some of them.

Instead she says, *Gu Ma*— and then stops. She should not, but the question comes unbidden. *Are you sure everything's going to be okay?*

The older woman shows no exasperation at being asked again, for the third time since breakfast. *Of course, right as rain*, she repeats, the intonation and phrasing of her response consistent as a fairy tale. *Why are you so worried?*

You hear so many things—

Don't listen to things.

I read on the Internet about someone dying. He had cancer and they gave him a new liver, but he died two days later. It turned out the liver was HIV positive.

The aunt laughs. *Maybe that might happen at a private clinic. Anything could happen there. At this hospital they choose good organs. When I was still on the work unit, we had to match the tissue samples very carefully, to make sure everything was compatible before the executions went ahead. The patients who came through us all made full recoveries.*

Sophia isn't sure she has understood correctly. *Executions?*

The condemned prisoners were tested several times, everyone on death row, until we found something suitable. So much work. We had to inject them with an anti-coagulant before they were shot.

I didn't—I thought it was car accidents, or brain death—in most countries, it's—

Is it? Well, not in China. Who wants to meet their ancestors with half their insides missing?

With a swoosh of relief, the traffic starts to move again. The aunt nudges the car forward, jaggedly overtaking. Sophia wonders if she already knew this. Half-remembered magazine articles about forged signatures on consent forms, men and women appearing in court with their jaws wired shut to prevent them from speaking out. Why did she think this had nothing to do with her?

The aunt seems to guess at what is bothering her. *You shouldn't feel guilty. These are all people who've done bad things. This way at least they can pay something back to society.*

But how— and again, her limited vocabulary trips her up. *How can someone in that position really consent? Did our heart, the one now in my husband's chest—* But there are no words in any language to ask such a question. She tries not to think about what a short wait they had for a match.

Don't think about it, says the aunt. *I knew a lot of comrades who were sent to work in the abattoirs during re-education. They stopped eating meat after that. It's best not to think about it.*

They are moving at speed now, the traffic suddenly smooth again. Buildings streak past, concrete slabs studded with neon signs. Between bright pink beauty parlour hoardings and homely restaurant names, familiar images appear: Starbucks, The Gap, Taco Bell, English names replaced by Chinese characters but still instantly recognisable. *I could go into a shopping centre and pretend I'm home*, she thinks.

For the first time since coming here, she allows herself to imagine their Tanjong Pagar flat, to put herself in it, safely back with Nicholas. Perhaps in just a few days—stepping out of the lift, with their luggage. Opening the familiar door. Her mother's domestic helper comes round twice a week to clean, so there'd be no dust, just the faint lemon scent of floor polish. They'd walk slowly through the rooms as if to reclaim possession. Turn on the air-conditioning. And then?

She has not experienced this since school: an event so ominous it becomes impossible to see beyond, the emptiness of afterwards, the quiet desolation of the day after your last exam. Relief, of course, but also a dull ache, an absence like a missing tooth.

The aunt is speaking again, something about messages to pass on to her mother, her cousins. This is a family visit, and now that the main complication is over, there are protocols to negotiate, souvenirs to be bought. Sophia nods at the right moments. She will do this, but already she knows this is all, these messages from the aunt are the last real contact they will have. The Chinese do not send cards at Christmas, so there is not even that. Will she call the aunt, if she and Nicholas find themselves back in Beijing at some point? Well, perhaps. It would depend on their schedule. So awkward for Nicholas, who doesn't speak a word of Mandarin.

They parallel park on a side street. A warden comes over and mechanically recites: *Ten yuan for the first hour, five for each subsequent half-hour.* The aunt cuts him off. *I'll give you twenty, just let me park here as long as I want.* They haggle and settle on twenty-five, and he'll keep an eye on the car for her.

It is not far to the hospital, but the walk there is littered with the usual hazards. Uneven pavements that end abruptly, drivers who treat traffic lights as no more than suggestions. At one point they have to step out onto the road because the entire pavement is taken up by a donkey cart, from which an old couple are selling watermelons. Sophia follows closely behind the aunt, trusting in her to navigate the hostile terrain.

The safety wall before the hospital entrance is covered in earnest graffiti, marker pen rather than spray paint: some slogans that mean nothing to Sophia, and a great many phone numbers. She'd vaguely assumed these were prostitutes advertising. Now, she realises most of them are preceded by the same single character: "shen". Kidney.

Something gives way around the level of Sophia's own kidneys, some kind of air lock that suddenly empties her body of air, the rush of it leaving her barely able to stand.

For a moment she cannot draw breath, and she must put a hand on the sliding doors to steady herself. Not now. Deal with this later. Her chin snaps up, and she makes the effort to pull herself upright.

She becomes aware the aunt has said something. *Pardon?*

I'll let you see him alone, says the aunt. Don't worry about me. I'll go and have a chat with Old Cheng. I'll come find you later.

Gu Ma—thank you. This seems inadequate, but the older woman nods firmly, reassuringly, and trots off into the depths of the hospital. Sophia watches her go, her legs so sturdy. Looking at her aunt's broad back, her mind fills with unexpected tenderness.

All the way up the stairs, Sophia studies the faces of everyone she passes, trying to work out who is grieving, who is hopeful, what each person must be longing for. There is something like a song growing inside her, a lightness that breaks gradually, step after step. By the time she reaches Nicholas's floor, she is humming. There is queasiness beneath this, the rumble of upset waiting to make itself known, but she is able to push it far down and skate over its surface. The nurses smile politely as they pass her in the corridor, and she decides they are not so bad after all, these girls.

When she opens the door, Nicholas is in bed, the television on, a scene so familiar that for a second she feels the jolting fear that nothing has changed. But no, she's been watching him all week through the glass window, blurry from anaesthetic, bandages around him. Now he is finally out of Intensive Care. Now she can approach.

He looks up when she comes in. *They warned me that the anti-rejection drugs might make me go a bit funny. In case I say anything strange. It's temporary.*

She cannot speak. Already he is becoming like his old self, confident, still, his dark blue eyes no longer vulnerable. There will be months of therapy and years of pills ahead, she knows, and nothing can be certain. Yet the air of fearfulness that cloaked them for months is dispelled. Light through grey clouds. She cannot possibly say anything to break the joy of this moment. What would be the point? What can they do now, either of them?

Gu Ma's here, she says. *She'll come and say hello in a bit. Maybe—when you feel up to it—we should take her out for dinner before we go home.*

Of course. His voice is smooth with politeness. *She's done so much for us.*

I'll ask her to pick a restaurant. She must know somewhere nice. So easy to slip into familiarity, discussing dinner venues.

A strange new animal has taken up residence inside Sophia, and she will have to learn to reach an accommodation with it. It only rears its head if looked at directly, but otherwise remains dormant, only noticeable from its cold weight against her gut. The whole of this grey city seems bound up in that weight. She suddenly wants, more than anything, to feel Nicholas's warmth along the length of her body.

How are you? she says, in a way that requires no answer. He smiles, and she abandons her chair to snuggle next to him. The bed is really too narrow to accommodate them both, but just for a moment she wants to remember the familiar way they fit together, her chin against his shoulder. This is better. She runs her fingertips over the valleys of his collarbone, convincing herself he is real. The thickest bandages have come off, and now there is only a swathe of gauze down the middle of his chest. She is careful not to go anywhere near it; the scar underneath is still very tender.

They stay like that, watching television. Nicholas must be feeling better, the remote control is in his hand and he is scrolling freely through the channels. She translates, but before she is halfway through a sentence he has flipped again. They see scraps of game shows, overcooked period dramas, and what appears to be a travelogue centred entirely on food.

He hovers for some time on an unusual chat show. It is outdoors, and the guest is on a hard chair, in handcuffs, his head shaven. *What is this?* says Nicholas.

It takes Sophia a few seconds to work it out. *They're interviewing death row prisoners before execution. Asking what they've done, why they did it.*

Nicholas laughs, a warm sound she hasn't heard for too long. *Brilliant. I'm surprised Jeremy Kyle hasn't thought of it.*

The interviewer is a youngish woman, very fashionably made-up—feathery cropped hair and a loose silky top. *Do you repent?* she is saying. *Are you even sorry?*

The man looks down, unable to meet her eye. *Of course I'm sorry.*

What would you say to the parents, if they were here? All those families?

And now Sophia recognises him. He has been on the front page of every newspaper, along with his colleagues— the men and women in charge of the company that cut their milk powder with melamine. They are national villains, after killing so many babies. No wonder the interviewer looks at him with such contempt.

Poor bastard, says Nicholas. *But why would anyone agree to this? I suppose he'll be languishing in his cell now. At least he got his fifteen minutes.* Sophia does not tell him that the programme is a repeat, that the man is already dead, executed by a bullet through the right side of his chest. *Always the right side,* the aunt said, *so as not to damage—*

Those innocent children! hectors the interviewer. *The only hopes of their families—no siblings, because of our unique national circumstances.* Such cruelty. A single tear glistens in the corner of an eye. She dabs it away, examines her fingertip.

We didn't mean to, says the man quietly. *We just wanted to cut costs to avoid bankruptcy. No one was meant to—*

His voice wisps away along with his face. Nicholas

has pressed the button, and they are now on a cooking programme. *Strange country,* he says. *Strange, strange country. I can't wait to get home.*

And they are silent again, watching the presenter demonstrate the preparation of Chongqing hotpot. Not that they will ever try this; within easy reach of the Tanjong Pagar flat, there are three restaurants that serve excellent Chongqing hotpot. Still, it is fun to watch. Sophia continues to rest her head against the side of Nicholas's chest, carefully avoiding the scar, enjoying the rise and fall of his torso and its ferocious thumping, as if something inside is struggling to get out.

Toronto

FOR THE SECOND morning in a row, she wakes up convinced someone is in the room with her. Was it a voice that roused her? A man's, gravelly and indistinct—she cannot remember the words. Yet the door is locked, and she is on the fourth floor, too high for intruders. She grips a corner of the flimsy curtain and rips it open like a Band-Aid. Nothing but the window sill, scummy with moss and cigarette butts, and beyond it the sun rising over the wide city.

She is motionless for a few minutes, waiting for her heart to settle. Just a fragment of dream slipping over the borders of sleep. It is boiling hot in this room, on the top floor of a hotel too cheap for air-conditioning, an oven of low ceiling and narrow walls. Her own country is hot, but not like this, not dry roasting heat without the relief of humidity, so you stifle instead of sweat.

Rationality returns, and she knows no one could possibly be hiding here. No point even looking under the bed. Her rucksack is still on the floor, clothes spilling from its throttled mouth, then the splayed-open book she was reading, a pizza box and three cans of Molson's Dry. One still sloshes when as she tosses it in the bin, and she has to resist the urge to sip. The last slice of pizza will do for breakfast. As she gnaws at it, the sandy pepperoni strikes a flint of memory: yes, that was last night.

Today must go better. She will do useful things, not wander along streets at random until exhaustion tugs her onto a bench in the Allan Gardens greenhouse, bedraggled beneath severe Victorian ironwork. She will buy shampoo, work out how much money she has left, try to make a plan. By the time she meets Aimée, she must be able to impersonate someone normal.

The bathrooms are shared. When she finally drags herself to the one down the corridor, two Indian girls are giggling and fixing each other's hair in front of the mirror. They ignore her muttered greeting as she shuffles around them. Perhaps she is a little too old to be staying somewhere like this, full of backpackers expecting to be supplied with a social life along with a bed for the night. She doesn't look like she's having enough fun.

Toronto's edges are too hard for the mood she is in. Every road junction is a precise right angle, and even the trees grow straight up, perfectly vertical. When she stands for too long by the side of the road, trying to work out which way is north, cars stop and wait patiently for her to cross. She yearns to find litter in the road, or someone as dishevelled as she is, but everything is well-ordered and well-fed.

The phone booth is a provocation. She intends only to put in the first few digits, to see how it feels, but as soon as she starts she has dialled the whole calling card code and then her home phone, all memorised at university and now so ingrained she doesn't need to think of the numbers for her fingers to find them. Ringing, and then her father, *Hello, hello, is that you?* and her mother, faintly, *Tell her we're not angry, we just want her to—*

Your mother says just come home. We won't be angry.

She is quiet, wondering what she'd hoped to gain from this.

We know you're in Canada, from the credit card. I check the account every morning. I just want you to know you don't have to worry about—

After she hangs up, she removes the MasterCard from her wallet and bends it back and forth until it snaps cleanly in two. She drops each half into a different trash can a couple of blocks apart, not even slowing down as she flicks them away. Now she has no means of buying a plane ticket back, but she will worry about that at some point in the future. By mid-afternoon she has done nothing but pace restlessly across the streets of the downtown grid, and still she manages to be late.

Aimée looks good, clear-skinned, exactly the same except her breasts are larger. Motherhood suits her. She waves away apologies and orders more cake, more coffee. They talk about the baby, mutual friends, the weather. Aimée asks why she is here in the middle of term, so abruptly, but doesn't push when she is evasive. It was right to seek Aimée out. She is a good enough friend not to ask too many questions, but not such a good friend that she will know the right questions to ask.

At five-thirty, they walk over to meet Aimée's husband Scott. Even at rush hour, no one seems in a hurry. They amble or stand relaxed, not anxious for their streetcars to arrive. The clean lines of buildings are like a drawing, the windows neatly inked in. *You live in such a beautiful city,* she tells Aimée, who nods in simple acknowledgement of the fact.

They reach the pub at the same time as Scott, who has a complicated harness arrangement strapped to his front. She has to lean across the baby for a stubbly hello kiss. The waiter shows them to a table where Scott and Aimée's other friends are already waiting. Not everyone has seen the baby, and they fuss over him while the waiter goes to fetch a high chair. *Is it all right that—* she says, gesturing, and Scott grins, *It's fine, the baby won't be having any beer.*

Everyone is introduced to her in a flurry, saying who they are and passing menus round. A lot of stubby, manly names like Chad and Jim. She tells the story of how she met Aimée in a hostel years ago, how they stayed in touch by e-mail and how she's been promising to visit Toronto for years before finally making it now. She doesn't mention that Scott and

Aimée had always offered her a sofabed previously but with the child, the timing is understandably bad.

It turns out they are all teachers, colleagues of Scott or Aimée's, or classmates from training college. She tells them about the education system in her own country, and they discuss whether it is better because more disciplined, or worse because less flexible. Without reaching a conclusion, they move on to the standardised tests that are being rolled out province-wide. She is happy to be part of this general conversation, pushing aside questions about why she is here. Travelling, just travelling with no objective.

When the waiter comes, she asks Scott to order for her. This is her first trip, he says, and so she must try poutine. This turns out to be chips—frites, they insist—and cheese curds, squeaky against her teeth. The crucial thing, they tell her, is the gravy must be hot enough to melt the cheese. She cannot finish her portion, and the waiter packs it in a styrofoam box for her, cheerfully predicting it'll be even better the next day, when the chips have absorbed the gravy.

The baby begins to cry, not loudly but enough to remind them how late it is. The next day is a holiday. There is some kind of march most of them are going on, and they invite her along. The goodbyes are protracted, even though they will meet again in less than twelve hours. One of the men gallantly offers to walk her home. She has to admit to having forgotten his name, which turns out to be Nate. He says he does not mind—he understands what it's like, meeting so many new faces at once.

Nate teaches Maths (he says "Math") to fifteen-year-olds. She makes a weak joke about differentiation and is relieved when he laughs. Mostly they talk about normal things. She notices some teenagers lounging aggressively in an alleyway, all of them taller than her, and is grateful to have Nate with her like a talisman, although in truth they do not even look in her direction.

They reach the hotel, which is next to an all-night ramen bar. They stand on the pavement surrounded by people eating noodles. He is vague about how much further he has to walk, and she worries she may have taken him out of his way. He seems unwilling to leave, and they linger over this and that. She finds herself volunteering that no one knows where she is, that she just walked away from her job one day and got on a plane. *But are you married? Children?* he says—*No? Then you're an adult with no obligations and you're free to do what you like.* She tries to explain that it doesn't work like that, at least where she comes from, but he is leaning into her and she thinks he might—but the kiss is just on her cheek, and then he is upright again, the warmth of him withdrawing.

I'll see you in the morning, she says, meaning it, having decided she will actually get up early and go to this thing she doesn't even know the purpose of. *Don't forget to put the poutine in the fridge, or the cheese will go strange*, he says, then bounces on his heel and leaves, waving jauntily over one shoulder. She thinks she hears him whistling.

This isn't the kind of hotel that has fridges in the rooms, so she balances the box on the sill where it is at least a few degrees cooler. She watches it for a moment, gleaming white against the fug of sweaty night, before pulling the curtain shut.

A few hours later, she jolts awake, her chest heaving as if against an invisible weight. It is at least a minute before the pressure lets up. There is definitely a voice, guttural sounds coming from uncomfortably close by.

Keep still, she thinks, like a child. *Be very still and the devil may not notice you.* Yet the noise is not a dream, solid enough that it pulls her into full wakefulness and she draws the curtain. Straw-coloured sunlight dribbles in, over her strewn clothes and the wreckage of her sheets. On the window sill is a black squirrel, a few inches from her face, frantically gnawing at a wodge of cheese curd. It has torn apart the plastic bag and box. Jerking its head between bites, it detects her and barks twice, peremptorily, then scurries a few feet down a drainpipe to its tree branch escape route, disappearing before she has time to release the breath she didn't realise she was holding.

By the time she has cleared up the gummy mess and got out of the shower, it has begun to rain. Not a cleansing storm, but the sort of drizzle that seems determined to seep on for hours. She is tempted to get back into bed with a book—no, Nate is expecting her. And she feels a fleck of enthusiasm for the march itself. She has never protested anything before.

After just a couple of days here, she can find the street corner without a map—how simple, their names, like co-ordinates on a graph: Yonge and Bloor, King and Spadina. Such a lot of people, milling good-naturedly. The brilliant red of Aimée's hair flashes out at her, and she sees them, Scott next to her brandishing the baby like a trophy.

Some faces she remembers from the night before, including Nate. They will be marching with the Union of Teachers. *What are we demonstrating against?* she asks, and they laugh as they explain this isn't a protest, just the annual Labour Day march, all the unions turning out to remind the fat cats who actually does the work in this country.

The start time passes and still they wait. She goes into Tim Horton's to pick up coffee and a doughnut, and Nate comes to stand in the queue with her. When they return, everyone is still standing stoically in the rain. The atmosphere is stolid, yet there are flashes of carnival. Aimée squeals and rushes to hug friends from other schools, while total strangers come up to Scott to compliment him on the baby.

There is a stir in the crowd ahead that ripples down and then they are moving. Behind them the union of musicians plays something stirring—Sousa? Someone thrusts a flag into her hand which she holds stiffly, like a tour guide, until the others encourage her to wave it in time to the music. They march along Queen Street—all furniture shops and sushi restaurants, turning residential away from the city centre. As the rain clears, people emerge from their houses to watch the parade go by, some bringing out lawn chairs to set up on the pavement.

Later, her recollections of the morning will be fragmentary—a young woman and toddler on an upstairs balcony, dancing and throwing flowers down. People dashing ahead when they spot a coffee shop, hustling the counter staff to pour faster before the parade leaves them behind. An Asian woman in a green suit, handing out flyers—*Kuroda for council member*—that have Scott muttering darkly about trying to steal the labour vote. She worries that someone will accuse her of hijacking the march, but nobody questions her right to be there.

She is unused to walking long distances, but the climate is mild and the crowd so full of energy she forgets she is moving at all, as if she remains still while buildings and streetlights flow past on either side of her. From time to time the rain starts again, and a flurry of umbrellas rises through the crowd. She finds herself laughing joyously, for no reason at all, and nobody around her finds this in the least bit odd.

After an hour and a half, maybe two, they have walked five or six miles. This end of town is definitely rougher. There is a sense of openness as the buildings drift apart from each other. She realises they are headed towards the lake.

She's not sure who started it, but suddenly everyone is singing "When the Saints Go Marching In" and she is too, amazed she remembers all the words. She never sings. The route narrows, like the end of a marathon. In a scatter of raindrops, they go through a grandiose arch into a fairground of some kind, set up on the lakeshore. *What is this place?* she asks, as someone announces the Union of Teachers through a megaphone and everyone on the stands applauds, as if they were a high school football team. *This is the Canadian National Exhibition*, someone explains to her, *and people on the march get in for free—a treat for the workers*. Aimée takes a picture of them all, grinning widely, the baby wrapped in the flag like a revolutionary hero.

The Exhibition consists of a few large sheds, animals and farm produce on display. Nobody is very keen on this, so they go straight to the food, ravenous from the walk. Their picnic table fills with plates of barbecued meat, grilled vegetable skewers, onions sliced and then deep fried so they blossom open. They eat and eat. The afternoon is formless. Nate insists she try something called a beaver tail—some sort of pancake. A spiky French teacher is designated beer monitor, and brings round after round of Samuel Adams to the table as they toss him banknotes. She loses track of how much she is spending and tries to count. Aimée asks if she is all right and she says yes, just confused by Canadian money.

They wander amongst the fairground booths. Some people can't hold their liquor and go home, others who couldn't get out of bed in time for the march join them now. They skip the rides—probably wisely, given how much they have eaten—and seek out the games. The boys take turns to compete against the Test Your Strength machine, joking about who is the manliest. Aimée hands the baby to Scott and takes the hammer, beating them all, but they insist the stall-owner rigged it for her. Nate spends a fearsome amount of money on crockery-smashing until he wins a giant panda toy.

As it grows dark, they head to the Annex for a nightcap. Giggling, they dash to catch a streetcar and cram in higgledy piggledy, the driver opening the rear doors so Scott can get the baby's stroller on board. A surprisingly short ride later, they are sitting at a long outside table bickering over menus, calling for more beer, more frites. She tells them about the squirrel that morning, and they laugh as though it is the best joke ever.

Halfway through her first glass, she knows she must leave and stands up, looking unsteady enough that no one tries to stop her. Nate offers to make sure she gets home safely. *Are you afraid I'll run away again?* she says, trying to smile. Her legs are all anyhow, and she must lean quite hard against his forearm to stay upright. *Why can't I be good?* she thinks. When they get to the hotel, Nate presents her with the stuffed panda and she invites him upstairs.

At dawn the next morning, she wakes suddenly but does not stir. There is a whisper of fear before she turns and sees Nate's broad, golden back, half-covered by a sheet. He smells healthy, like laundry drying in the sun. She touches his dense, oil-black hair as gently as she can and whispers his name, then lies back down, carefully, watching for any sign of movement. She intends just to stay there looking at him, but her eyes drift shut, contentedly. When she wakes again later that morning, he is gone.

Harmonious Residences

THEY FOUND HIS decapitated body on the forty-first floor.
Earlier, his head had travelled down in the lift and rolled out
to meet two startled showroom girls, who had come in early
to preen themselves before the first customers. They became
understandably hysterical and had to be given the rest of the
day off, which would have been quite inconvenient if the
police hadn't closed off the site.

Foul play was suspected until closed-circuit footage from
inside the lift showed no one present apart from the man
himself, staying back late to finish a particular job—nobody
knew what, there were so many things to be taken care of
every day. His hands full, he tried to stop the lift doors with
his head, but a sensor was faulty and the doors kept closing,
trapping and then severing his neck.

I was on secondment to the Housing Development Board
at the time, and had been sent down to the site as a kind of
floating officer. These placements were usually uneventful,
but I knew this incident would be seen as a test for me.

Harmonious Residences was supposed to be a flagship project, an Executive Condominium with the kind of sleek, imposing design that wins architectural awards. It was in nobody's interest for the new buildings to seem unsafe.

Mercifully, press reception the next day was sombre rather than outraged. The blood had been cleaned up as soon as the police left, so the photographs showed nothing more gruesome than an ordinary lift landing—even if it was, as *The New Paper* insisted on calling it, "An Elevator to Death".

The deceased was a construction worker from China, surname Chen. Not much was known about him; we don't keep files on these people. "At least there's no family to make a fuss," said Li Hsia. When I pointed out that he must have one somewhere, she amended that to: "No family with access to the media."

Li Hsia was also a scholar. The HDB had sent her to Oxford to read Geography, and now she was on a fast-track to the top. She would clearly not be spending much longer hanging around construction sites, but the Party always makes you spend a bit of time getting to know people on the ground before you leave them behind, so if you do well enough to stand for election you can claim to have grassroots support.

She was quick off the mark, as expected, and arrived at work having already drafted a press statement on her Blackberry. Meanwhile, I was showing the police around and trying to get things back to normal. It was agreed that the chain of unfortunate events was clear enough and, there being nothing to investigate, we would start work again the next day. Of course, no one would use the lift until it had been safety-inspected.

None of us wanted to talk to the workers, until finally Soong volunteered. They seemed to like him—some evenings he kicked a football around the site with them, not something I could imagine myself doing. He spoke to them in his disjointed English, a pidgin simple enough for them to understand, reassuring them this was no more than a freak accident. They probably didn't miss Chen; he was too new to have made friends yet.

Things had just got back to normal when Mr Seetoh phoned, ordering me to meet the widow. "Your Chinese is not too bad, right? It's okay, you won't have to say much." I imagined his round face with the phone clamped under one ear, ticking my name off his list of tasks. Before I could say yes or no, he had hung up, my assent assumed.

I was reluctant to go through something so potentially awkward, and tried to persuade Li Hsia to take my place, but she was busy dealing with Minister. There were bound to be more questions asked, in Parliament and by the press, and he had to have all the facts at his fingertips, as well as reassurances that the launch would not be delayed. She waved me away, preoccupied with the dossier she was compiling.

Mrs Chen turned out to be older than I imagined, or perhaps she hadn't slept since hearing the news. She had come directly from the airport and was still clutching her luggage, an old trolley bag and various parcels. I hadn't had time to prepare for this, and found myself running through my repertoire of condolences far too quickly. My Mandarin vocabulary was mostly culled from local TV serials, fortunately replete with many death scenes.

In the face of her eerie silence, my monologue sputtered and stammered to a halt. Had she even understood me? People talk differently in China. In desperation, I started to ask if she wanted a glass of water when she said, not looking at me, "I want to see his body."

"I'm sure that can be arranged," I said unsteadily, then remembered we were supposed to promise nothing. "I mean, possibly. I don't know if they'll need to carry out an inquest."

"Where did he die?"

I mechanically pointed at the block where it happened, and described the circumstances in some detail. Fault couldn't possibly be attributed to our organisation; we operated under the most stringent safety regulations and he should never have been up there on his own. Searching for a positive note to end on, I managed, "He died without any pain."

"How do you know? Were you there?"

"No, of course not, Mrs Chen, no one was. That's why it happened."

"So he died all alone."

"Unfortunately."

"What will happen next?"

Glad to be on safer ground, I began to explain about the compensation structure. He hadn't been working very long for us, so it wouldn't be as high as it could be, but there would be some provision for his family.

She interrupted me. "I'm talking about his body."

I blinked, finding this in bad taste. "He'll be burnt"— I was momentarily unable to remember the Mandarin for "cremated"—"in the next few days, once the coroner is satisfied."

"No."

"We have to follow the procedure."

"He will come with me."

"Mrs Chen," I tried to soften my tone by imagining she was my mother. "You can't possibly bring the body back to China. It would cost far too much. Let us deal with this, and you can take the ashes back with you."

"You can't do this to him."

"It's out of our hands." And that seemed to be the end of it. Once the conversation moved onto ascribing blame, it was relatively simple for me to deflect it in other directions. The lift manufacturers, the various Ministries with a hand in this—though I stopped short of pointing the finger at Chen himself, even though to my mind he was every bit the author of his own misfortune.

She continued to be silent, and I considered that enough time had passed for our interview to come to a natural end. I stood up and headed purposefully for the door. "It was good of you to come and see us, Mrs Chen. I'm glad I had the chance to speak with you. Do you know where you're putting up?"

Without answering, she walked through the door I was holding open for her. I said something to cover the silence, and watched as she marched into the blazing sun, her bag trailing on the uneven ground. I thought of shouting goodbye, but it was far too noisy—all the machinery was once more going full pelt, the pile-driving for Phases 3 and 4 thump-thumping away even as we put the finishing glosses on the first two blocks.

"How was it?" While I was preoccupied, Li Hsia had come up behind me. I knew it was her before she spoke—unlike the sweaty bodies on site, she smelt faintly of oleander all day. When I turned, she was looking at me with an expression halfway between amusement and concern.

"Not too bad. She's upset, of course."

"I'm sure it's all right. We just needed to meet her, to show we care."

"I guess I'm not used to dealing with members of the public."

"Public?" She smiled. "Wait till you're really dealing

with the public, then you'll know the meaning of the word 'difficult.' Foreign workers don't count. Who are they going to complain to?"

"I don't think I was very helpful, though."

"What are you going to do, bring her husband back to life?" She looked narrowly at me. "Calvin, you mustn't care so much. You didn't cause the accident, I don't understand why you're feeling so guilty. These things happen."

Her callousness was bracing. I found myself wanting to be like her, with her certainty and confidence. Everything she said was true—I couldn't argue with her. It wasn't my fault.

"So what if she's not happy? Do you think she's going to *blog* about it?"

"Her husband's dead," I protested.

"That's very sad, but we can't stop everything because of one man."

"Do you want to have lunch with me?"

A defensive colour entered her eyes, and I knew I had mistimed this somehow. Asked her at the wrong point in the conversation, or sounded too keen. Perhaps, as a pretty girl, she was always on the alert for invitations that carried too much meaning.

"I'm just going to eat at my desk. They want the revised schedule breakdown by this afternoon." She smiled, softening the blow, and touched my forearm. "But another time, okay?"

I watched as she walked away. She was a few years younger than me, and already so sure of herself that the last few moments had felt completely natural, as if nothing at all awkward had taken place. I already knew that the next time I saw her, neither of us would mention this, and her manner to me would be as cheerful as ever.

My head badly needed clearing, so I decided not to seek out anyone else but to go for lunch on my own. There were a few food courts and coffee shops nearby—one of the estate's selling points was its proximity to these outlets—and I knew that if I left now, it was unlikely I would run into any of my colleagues. As I walked through the gates, I noticed Mrs Chen across the road, struggling to get all of her bags onto a bus. She did not look in my direction.

■ ■ ■

Soong's distorted face looked pained as he shouted rather than sang into the microphone, but his audience seemed to appreciate it. He was gripping the mike in both hands, his hair floppy with sweat. I have never seen the appeal of karaoke, but on this occasion had agreed to go with the flow because everyone from the office would be there. Although usually self-sufficient, on days like this one I felt the need of company.

The funeral had been earlier that afternoon. As a mark of respect, the site was closed so all the workers who wanted to could go—and of course, those of us in the office had to turn up as well. No one had thought to bring clothes to change into afterwards, and we must have made a strange group, turning up to the bar all in dark colours, the men in ties and the women with hair slicked demurely back.

Nobody was feeling good after the proceedings of that afternoon. We had filed into a vast wooden hall in Mandai crematorium, and it was immediately clear that someone had booked the wrong room. This was far too big for the dozen or so of us, defensively clumped together on just a couple of the benches, making the space look even more dauntingly empty. Mrs Chen sat some distance off, ostentatiously alone. Some of the workers spoke to her afterwards in their rough, kind way, and Mr Seetoh said something during the ceremony, but she knew no one in this country and made us all feel it.

Later, in the viewing gallery, I couldn't shake off the feeling that we were somewhere unnatural, like an alien church. The high ceilings and sheer granite walls of the building loomed in all directions, presumably intended to give the occasion stature, vast and comfortless. I drew an involuntary breath when the doors opened and the coffin glided cleanly into the aperture behind it.

Soong's discordant voice, heartbreakingly out of tune, dragged me from my thoughts. His last note, hoarse and flat, stretched out longer than the music. He got a respectable round of applause as he sauntered back to his seat, and a couple of the sillier showroom girls simpered at him. He had the casual swagger of the man who knows it is in the delivery and not the tune that hearts are won.

Li Hsia, I was glad to see, appeared indifferent to these antics, and was speaking soberly to Mr Seetoh about whether the office ought to send flowers to the widow, as a gesture of goodwill. I approached to ask what they wanted to drink, and then slipped outside to order. When I came back, Mr Seetoh was at the mike belting out something in Cantonese. I took the opportunity to slip into his seat.

"You're not singing?" said Li Hsia. She herself had been one of the first up, drifting tunefully through something by Adele before declaring she knew no other songs.

"I can't sing," I responded. She seemed to accept this, and I knew for sure she was different from the other girls, the ones who would have urged me to try, be a sport, have a go—Li Hsia left me to myself, and sipped at the dregs of her orange juice.

"What made you choose Geography? To study, I mean," I said, after the silence had grown dense. I was on my third bottle of beer and fuzzy around the edges.

She shrugged. "No reason. It was my best A-Level subject."

"Did you expect to end up here?"

"In a karaoke bar?"

"On a construction site."

"I don't mind it. I've met a lot of interesting people." She flashed a smile at one of the better-looking sales staff, squeezing past us on his way to the toilet.

I leaned in as if I couldn't hear her above the noise of the singing. Casually, my hand found her forearm. She didn't react, apart from just as casually angling her body a little away.

"Harmonious Residences," I said.

"What about it?"

"I like the name."

"I don't think it's anything special."

I was saved from having to explain by the waitress arriving. She bent herself expertly to fit into the tight space, and laid our drinks out just so—the coasters parallel to each other, not spilling a drop of the icy liquid. I murmured thanks but she seemed not to hear me, focussing entirely upon her task. She was thin and very young, I realised, and looked utterly exhausted.

Li Hsia toyed with her straw, and I decided it was up to me to ask another question. "Do you like working with us?" She smiled vaguely, not bothering to answer. "With me," I should have said.

"What books do you like reading?"

"What?"

"Books. You."

She shrugged, still smiling. I couldn't work out if she still hadn't heard me, or thought this was too odd a question. I took a pull from my beer bottle, wishing one of us was close to finishing so I could offer to go to the bar again.

"He's quite good." I indicated Mr Seetoh, currently bobbing along with his eyes shut, unfazed by a long instrumental interlude. "I didn't know he spoke Cantonese."

"Do you know him well?"

"No, I only met him on this project."

She nodded again, graceful and contained. The room was not large, and all around us I was aware, despite the gloom, of the other warm bodies contained in it. One of the girls had actually fallen asleep. For all the people just a few inches from us, I felt enveloped in something claustrophobic and sticky, thickening in the air between Li Hsia and me.

"We should come out and have a drink sometime. I mean, just us. The two of us." The English language was growing clumsy on my tongue. I thought how much more elegantly I could have put that in German. Uns beide. Or even in Chinese.

She nodded, vaguely, non-committal enough to avoid rudeness without giving anything away. She seemed to be scanning the air to the left of my head, hoping something would turn up, and it was from there that I heard Mr Seetoh's voice.

I jumped up. "I'm in your seat," I began automatically to apologise, relieved someone else had flattened the jagged silence between us.

"Hock," said Li Hsia, looking at him. "I think we should go."

"So soon?"

"I'm tired."

He grunted and, without taking his eyes off me, tossed her the keys. "You drive." A breath of perfume as she stood up. He continued to stare, but his tone was friendly. "Lucky she doesn't drink. Such a good girl. Useful to have someone to take me home."

My throat was too dry to construct a useful reply, but I think I managed to nod fitfully.

"See you at work, Calvin." He patted me on the shoulder. "Bright and early."

I watched them walk away, wondering if she would turn back and smile at me. Not a meaningful smile, just something kind to take the sting out of the evening. She didn't, of course, she looked only at him. As they slipped through the door, I saw the tired waitress leaning against the corridor wall, her broom and tray beside her. As soon as we left, she would swoop in to erase the night's mess as quickly as possible.

As the door closed, I noticed Soong glancing slyly at me. He whispered something to the girls beside him, and they giggled like monkeys. I ignored them as best I could, sat back down and picked up my beer. I would give them time to get clear, and then leave. It wouldn't take long, the car park was only one floor up. Five minutes. I began counting to three hundred in my head.

■ ■ ■

Mrs Chen came back to Harmonious Residences the night of the funeral. Dressed in old clothes and carrying a large Styrofoam box, she convinced the night watchman she was a drinks seller, and he let her in. This would cost him his job, because the site was meant to be secure at night—but the men wanted food and drink, and were often too tired to go out to get it. As soon as she was out of sight of the entrance, she slipped round the side of the building, and punched in the security code she must have watched me entering that other day. The office had no alarm, and she was able to walk right in with no trouble. We found all this out much later, at the trial.

By the time the site supervisor called me, it was just after five in the morning and pitch black. I was lying face down on my bed, fully dressed. I briefly considered leaving just as I was, but that was too disgusting even for the way I felt, and I stopped to shower and change. The dull throbbing in my head would certainly become unbearable by lunchtime. I slipped some paracetamol in my pocket and left the flat, careful not to wake anyone else.

I had never had a reason to take the MRT so early in the

morning—I got on the first train, the sky just lightening, and was surprised how few people were about. At some stations no one got on or off, and the doors did no more than a perfunctory shuffle. Everyone looked cold and tired, although no one quite as ill as I felt. I began working out the quickest way I could get hold of some coffee.

When I arrived at the construction site, everything was still, almost peaceful. With the great machines at rest, without noise and dust swirling around everything, it was possible to see the buildings as their true selves, magnificent. In a few months, defiled by human habitation, they would become commonplace: stained by polluted rain, sprouting laundry on bamboo poles and unmatched curtains from every window. But now, the first motes of sun just landing on their long glass surfaces, they stood proud of their surroundings like monuments, like tall and silent gods.

The security post was empty and I walked straight in, mechanically making a mental note to mention it later. They had told me where Mrs Chen was, but I felt the need to go to my office first, if only as a matter of routine. Entering the showroom, it became clear that Mrs Chen's visit had not been a peaceful one. She had smashed everything breakable in the room—and there were many things, many mirrored surfaces intended to make the space look bigger. Because Minister insisted on creating a gracious ambience to reflect our cultured society and sophisticated clientele, we'd engaged a local interior design firm to dot delicate lamps and vases about the room, now so much crushed coloured glass.

Picking my way through the scarred furniture, I was struck by how little this mattered. I would make some phone calls, and in half a day everything would be put to rights. Perhaps not all the objets would be replaced, but the debris would be expertly cleared, and we would be able to admit members of the public by lunchtime. For all her destructive efforts (achieved, we later found out, with no more than a hammer from a stray toolbox), Mrs Chen had gained nothing permanent.

There was nothing to be done here, for the time being, and I made my way up the tallest tower, the one they were holding her in. The lift glided up the outside of the building on smooth treads, until I was clear of the surrounding clutter and could see the view our lucky residents would be paying a premium for, as yet unimpeded by other buildings. I never grew tired of this, the green sweep of East Coast Park and the sea beyond. It was a fine thing in Singapore to look out and see only earth and water, not people.

When the doors opened on the forty-first floor, I saw Mrs Chen on a plastic stool, the security guard's hand firmly on her shoulder. It hardly seemed a necessary precaution; she clearly had no fight left. She was slumped, barely upright, her hands and head limp as though her neck were broken. All around her was chaos, the walls defiled and the floor thick with debris. The guard nodded at me, as did the short Malay policewoman just putting her notebook away.

"She doesn't want to tell us anything. Do you know why she did this?"

"Her husband," I said.

"Yes, I know, sir, we read the papers too," she had a patient voice, but was clearly very tired, perhaps at the end of her shift. "But it was an accident, right? And she's getting compensation?"

"Maybe. We still have to have a tribunal to prove it wasn't his own negligence." Suddenly I was tired of my voice. How could anyone possibly explain why this had happened? Mrs Chen would say nothing all the way through her trial, and remain silent as they sent her to prison. She'd already said all she possibly could.

"She refused to move from here. We're waiting for another officer to assist."

"Her husband died here," I explained. "On this floor."

She nodded. "Do you know what this means, sir?" She was pointing at the walls, which were covered with wild slashes of paint (the Styrofoam box, it emerged, had been full of spray paint—the guard had heard the clanking metal, but assumed it was drink cans). They were Chinese characters, not all of which I recognised. Chen's name. Something about retribution. Some dates. It was a statement of something, or maybe her story. I would have to ask Soong about it later.

Thinking of Soong brought me back to what was in store for me later, after last night. Soong was incapable of subtlety, and what he thought of as innuendo would no doubt be crude and broad enough to ensure the whole office knew what had happened in the bar. I would deny it, of course, but people notice things, and I had been looking at Li Hsia a certain way all week.

"Sir?" said the policewoman. She was waiting for me to translate the writing for her. I didn't want to admit my Mandarin wasn't good enough to decipher the rant of the woman from China, and took a guess. It was about the circumstances of her husband's death, I told her. It was about a man who came to this country to earn money and ended up dead.

The policewoman nodded. "But we heard all that at the inquest, sir. I remember reading about it. My colleague gave evidence. It was very sad, but these things happen." She gestured around her. "I don't understand people like this. Why would she do such a thing? How will she remember him now?"

It was then that I realised the dust we were standing in was not dust. We were in a pool of small grey particles, dotted with charred white lumps. She had tipped her husband's ashes out onto the very spot where he met his end, and when the lift doors opened for me, some of it had blown in. We would never get all of it out, it was so fine. There would always be a little of him here.

"She must be crazy," the policewoman was saying. "Why do these people behave like this? When my father died I was sad, but I didn't behave like this. These people don't understand."

And it made sense to me, just at that moment, why you would want to leave your husband here, in this strange land, and not bring any of him back with you. I understood, but there was no way I could have told her any of this, I didn't have the right words. Already I was thinking: I am in the wrong place. There is nothing for me to do here. I should go downstairs, where there is coffee, and normalcy, and the day can begin as usual. It will be a difficult morning, but the fuss over the destroyed showroom will distract Soong from mischief. Li Hsia, graceful as always, will pretend nothing happened last night. I will be all right, I thought. Everything will be all right.

I told the policewoman I needed to get the clear-up underway. She nodded. She had the situation under control. I pressed the button for the lift and we waited, awkwardly, until it arrived. At the faint ding of the bell, Mrs Chen's head jerked up, her lips silently twitching. She looked straight at me with the wild stare of a cornered animal, trapped and furious, bright with helpless energy. Her eyes were no longer human. I backed slowly into the lift, but could not break her gaze until the doors slid shut between us.

Stray

THE FRIEND WHO lent Li Hsia the Bangkok flat warned her not to leave the sinks unplugged. "I used to get cockroaches, not many, maybe a couple each month. None since I started doing this." It gave her a queasy feeling every time she had to lift a stopper to brush her teeth or wash a cup. As if there might be a fat brown roach lurking in the pipes, waiting to shove its nasty bulk through the plughole at the first chink of light. She kept one hand positioned above the tap, ready to drown the bastard if necessary.

The flat was smaller than she had expected, no more than a glorified bedroom with a toilet attached, on the top floor of a squat concrete building full of similar shoeboxes. No lift, but at least there was a reasonable view of the city's scattered skyscrapers. It was a short walk to the BTS station, and her friend assured her that in a few minutes she could be back in civilisation.

Her presence here was one of those coincidences only possible in the age of the Internet. Skimming Facebook whilst watching television one night, she'd noticed her photographer friend Sam—really, an acquaintance, someone she'd been at university with—mention heading back to London for his first solo show. On a whim she dropped him a message asking what would happen to his flat, and by the next day they were making plans for her to take over the place.

Her colleagues were unsurprised when she announced she was going. Officially, she had a lot of leave stored up, like a good workaholic, needing to be used by the end of the year. Everyone knew what had really happened, and it was understandable that she would want to hide her face for a while. Nobody was unsympathetic, exactly, but Li Hsia was not the sort of person who inspired warmth. She knew they all thought she had been asking for it, that it was just a matter of time, and the worst of it was that they were right.

She was used to travelling light, and arrived at Suvarnabhumi Airport with just a small suitcase, like an air hostess. It was only a couple of hours from Singapore, and she could always go back if she had forgotten anything crucial. The keys were with a neighbour, Allan, who turned out to be a sturdy, shortish American, maybe forty, with a goatee and one earring.

"How long are you in Bangkok?" he asked, leaning in his doorway.

"A month." She was polite, but careful not to say too much. No sense encouraging superfluous friendships.

"Sam didn't think he'd find anyone to sublet for such a short time."

"It's just right for me. Cheaper than a hotel."

"Well, enjoy it. Knock on the wall if you need anything." His shoulder still slouched against the doorjamb, he leaned forward to shake her hand.

The windows were painted shut, presumably to keep mosquitoes out, so she had the air-conditioning on all the time. Her first evening there, she went to the 7-Eleven and found some surprisingly edible reheatable rice-and-curry dishes. She filled Sam's fridge with food and bottled water. She could stay in for days, if necessary. That first evening she ate greedily, heating packets of fried noodles and chicken chunks in sweet sauce. She would allow this, a few days of sloth, perhaps gaining some weight and letting her hair go greasy.

The practical part of her wanted to find a purpose, to not waste this month. It should feel like a gift to herself, an entire thirty days given over to emptiness, no work, no family. She knew no one in Bangkok and didn't speak the language. Her e-mail was set to automatically rebuff all enquiries ("Li Hsia is away till the end of the month. If your message is urgent, please contact" and then the names of two other people in her department). The flat seemed to hum with a sense of protectiveness, a capsule with just her in it, adrift in the wide world.

Sam had left her the number of his cleaner, but she decided not to call. It wasn't the money, a few dollars a week; she just felt odd about having someone come in to clean a space this small. She was happy to do it herself; it took about ten minutes to sweep everywhere, including under the bed. She wondered briefly if she was depriving this woman of her income for the month, but shrugged the thought away. You can't worry about everyone.

She drew up a timetable—a swim first thing in the morning, a jog in the evening—then laughed at her earnestness. There were too many hours in the day to fill. It demanded a big project, maybe learning a language or knitting a cardigan, but she wasn't ready to commit to anything that large. For now she was happy to work her way through Sam's shelves, full of the sorts of books she had always meant to read. How had they drifted apart so easily after university, she wondered, when their tastes were so similar? It was a pleasant surprise when he decided to set up a studio in Thailand, so close to her in Singapore, but they never managed to find the time to meet.

The walls of the flat were papered with poster-sized prints of Sam's work. Some of them had been taken from these very windows, representing Bangkok as a fallen futuristic city, tall twisted towers arising from the jungle. Others were of clouds, the moon, street corners. None of them contained people, as if Sam had decided human beings were not a worthy subject.

It unsettled her, waking up to these blotches of colour, blown up beyond their natural size. Eventually she covered them with the spare bedsheet.

By and large, she managed to drift quite pleasantly, letting one hour slip by, and then another, until it became time for a meal. Perhaps this was what is meant by "living in the present". It was only at bad moments that unwelcome thoughts pressed into her mind, the sweet nightmare of the last year. Such a clever woman, falling into cliché and sleeping with her manager, the whole office knowing. And then the chill of being left. Now he swept off to lunch without even looking at her, and she had to go to the staff canteen like everyone else. As soon as she got back, she decided, she would apply for a transfer to a different department. She would probably get it—she interviewed well, and had the sort of CV that catches the eye.

Although she tried not to go out when there were footsteps on the stairs, inevitably she ran into Allan and his Thai girlfriend on the landing, arriving with armfuls of shopping just as she was locking up. "Going out?" he said, amiable, and she nodded, even though she was only heading down to put the remains of her dinner in the communal bin.

"You spending this whole month here in Bangkok?"

She nodded again, and then feeling that more might be required of her, added, "I like to get to know a city really well. To experience living there."

He smiled lazily, mentally bracketing her alongside himself, one of nature's drifters. A traveller, not a tourist. She managed to imply with her eyes that she had somewhere urgent to be, and scuttled apologetically down the stairs, feeling the glare of the Thai girlfriend at her back. Allan hadn't introduced them.

Just in case he asked her the next time they met, she felt she should go somewhere. An expedition. She allowed herself the decadence of an afternoon movie at Siam Paragon, but that was just like Singapore, a multiplex inside a giant shopping centre. After the film she walked along the glittering passageways. It was exactly the same: Topshop, River Island, Giordano. Even on a weekday afternoon the building was crowded, full of people wandering as if dazed by visions of plenty, carrying Abercrombie and Fitch carrier bags printed with athletic American torsos. She had a Starbucks coffee and felt like an international fraud.

She knew she ought to make an effort, visit a floating market or a temple, but the idea of organising this exhausted her. She rode the skytrain to the end of the line, a bubble gliding over the rooftops of Bangkok. It was a patchy city, some bright new buildings, but also many old ones that desperately needed repainting. Walking back to her flat, she noticed courtyards and corners encrusted with plastic bags and dirt.

Every street she walked down smelt faintly of sewage. And

yet the Thai people themselves were fastidious, always neatly turned out. The BTS at rush hour, even on the hottest day, did not contain the humming stink of tired bodies pressed close together, as subway trains in other cities always seemed to. She was taking more and more trains now, pressing herself into the crowds of the city. As long as she stayed silent, no one knew she didn't belong here.

At night she stayed indoors, watching Thai television without understanding a word of it, cleaning the flat. It became a game, a challenge to herself, to find and eliminate patches of dirt. She was starting to acclimatise, but still found herself wanting to clean the whole city when she was out. Why were great heaps of rubbish left to moulder in the streets? When it rained, black water sloshed out of the drains and slurred more dirt across the pavements. It all needed a good scrub, every inch of it. She battled away at the flat, hand-washing curtains and polishing tiles until her body was slick with sweat, and then cleaning herself with equal diligence.

Sometimes faint sounds came through the walls, voices and cries as if from far away. Was Allan fighting with the Thai girl, or were they watching a film? She saw them around the neighbourhood sometimes, in one of the small local restaurants or on their way to the BTS. The girl usually looked sullen, tiny next to the American's broad shoulders, dressed like a child in little blouses and jewelled slippers.

Perhaps she wasn't just preternaturally young-looking, like most Thai women, but actually thirteen years old.

Later on, when the neighbourhood was quiet, she felt the flat settle into itself. It was soothing, the way you could see every inch of it from the bed. She liked to creep around its perimeter, tracing the walls and furniture with her hands. It was somewhere between a sanctuary and a prison, like an anchorite's cell. What would it be like to stay here forever? Thailand was such a cheap country that she could feasibly spend a decade here before her savings ran out.

The small pool at the back of the apartment complex turned out to be unusable, scummy with leaves and disuse. Although she was careful not to swallow any of the water, a sour taste lingered in her mouth for hours afterwards, no matter how many times she brushed her teeth. The grounds here were littered with stray cats, scrawny specimens that meowed insolently as she walked past. She wondered if they pissed in the water.

She began jogging at night, after the sun had set and the air turned less stifling. Many of the roads had no pavements, and often no pedestrian crossings either. She picked routes that stayed away from traffic. It felt good, the jolt of her feet on the ground, the last shreds of heat from the day. She sang half-remembered verses of Cantopop songs, happy to be ridiculous with no one nearby to hear. The rhythm of her steps was far too fast for this song. Once she tried Lumphini

Park, but it stank with danger after dark, shifty figures in the undergrowth. She went back to the roads.

Every night she pushed herself a little further, and by the end of the second week was penetrating quite far into the estate. Turning a corner, she came up against two of the large feral dogs that roamed the streets. She stopped and they stared at each other. She knew better than to offer her hand, they would not be making friends. Another dog nosed its way out of the undergrowth and came up behind her. She was surrounded now. She should have kept jogging, when she had momentum on her side.

Was she really in danger? There were four of them now, and then five, unmoving, lips pulled back from their teeth. She knew she had to keep her movements calm, but as she stepped down from the curb she stumbled and pitched forward an involuntary couple of steps, and they jerked towards her as a mass. Don't run, the worst thing you can do is to show your fear. She forced herself to move forward, casually. They kept pace with her, watchful.

It was like a nightmare of wading through soft mud, of weighed-down feet unable to escape from the monster. She made her breath even, tried not to imagine teeth sinking into the soft flesh of her calf, dragging her to the ground where they could finish her off at their leisure. She found herself murmuring his name under her breath, her lover— whispering his name like a talisman, a habit she was trying to wean herself off. As if he could help her now. As if he would notice.

She had moved only a few metres, and wondered how long it would be before they lost patience and lunged. No one knew where she was. Would they be able to identify her body? Afraid of being mugged, she usually kept her pockets empty except for keys. Now she wished she had something, at least her name on a scrap of paper, anything to keep her corpse from being anonymous. She would languish unclaimed in the morgue for weeks, and probably be in a pauper's grave by the time Sam got round to reporting her missing.

The road was poorly lit, and she navigated it in tight steps, terrified of losing her footing. If she stumbled…but she would not. She would keep her head up, chest forward, confidence holding them at bay. Her feet teetered along the tightrope of street markings, obscured every few feet by puddles. She did not need to look down to know the animals were still there, all around her.

She was so focussed on moving that she did not immediately register the roar of an engine, and then a motorcycle came round the corner and screamed towards them. The dogs scattered before it could hit them, yelping, suddenly like beaten children. For a heartbeat of stillness, she registered their ribs as they fled—literally, turned tail—how thin and mange-ridden their coats were. And then she was running, her heart about to burst, gulping air and not stopping until she could see the lights of the main road.

Pedestrians looked at her curiously as she lurched down Sukhumvit. No one ran here except the farang, foreigners. Her legs bowed with terror and exhaustion but she couldn't stop, had to keep going, somewhere between a stoop and a stumble. Why had she never noticed before how many strays prowled the streets? The grimy pavement seemed a parade of threats, now her balance was disturbed. Loose paving stones. Food stalls and their woks of boiling oil on shaky charcoal burners. She clutched her elbows to her chest, occupying as little space as possible.

When she got back to her building, Allan and his girlfriend were in the carpark, doling out a gummy mixture of rice and fish from a packet. Around them at least half a dozen cats crouched, gnawing intently as if the food might disappear at any moment.

"Lisa, hey," called Allan. "Good evening?" She managed to nod, even force a smile. He shrugged at the animals around his feet. "They break your heart, cats," cuffing one mock-viciously, grinning to show it was a joke. "Still. She loves them." The girlfriend was making cooing noises and stroking their piebald heads as they ignored her, emitting little grunts and mews as they chewed. Allan looked as if he were ready to go back indoors, but she seemed determined to stay and make sure they finished every scrap.

The flat seemed smaller when Li Hsia stepped inside it, aware for the first time of a faint stale smell. She double-locked the door, shoving the deadbolt firmly home, and checked that the plugs were in place in the sinks and shower. Dashing round the room, she clattered shut the mosquito screens and thick blinds, making sure they covered the whole of the windows, corner to corner. Only then did she realise she had been holding her breath, and let it out in a shaky gasp that rattled in her throat. When she turned out the light, the darkness was total.

Meatpacking

SHE SEES A group of them, young ones, huddled around a laptop, and knows immediately what it will be. There is something recognisable about them, a sense of like calling to like. Sure enough, as she gets closer, the tinny music grows familiar, the same songs they've been playing since her childhood. She should turn, walk the other way, but something draws her further into the café, a studenty joint, not her usual sort of place.

There are six of them, five boys and a girl, all in sloppy T-shirts, dirty jeans and plastic-rimmed glasses. Undergraduates, probably; this side of St Mark's Place is lousy with them. They are gazing fixedly at the MacBook Air on the table, angled for optimal viewing, hooked up to small but powerful speakers.

On the screen, a phalanx of schoolchildren in sunflower yellow are singing tunelessly, their voices kept from straying too far off-piste by a humourless brass band. The Combined Schools Choir, her brain whispers unbidden. It was her job one year to supervise rehearsals, two of her classes having been forcibly volunteered to take part. She remembers the sweaty late-afternoon stillness, waiting for the event to start—how unnatural it was for a large space in the city centre to be so silent.

She realises the undergrads are looking at her. She must have been staring for too long, too closely. Just as she is about to smile apologetically and move on, one of them addresses her. *Singaporean, is it? You Singaporean or Malaysian?*

Must be Singaporean, says the girl. *Must be. Malaysian where got interested?*

You want to watch? says another one. *Come, never mind, sit with us, the Wi-Fi here damn fast, shiok.*

She stares at them, wondering if this is a performance for her benefit, if they have coarsened their grammar and dialled up the Singlish as—what? A claim of authenticity? A provocation? *I'm not*— she begins, *I'm from*— But that is enough for her accent to expose her, for them to exchange knowing looks. Confirmation.

Don't shy, says the first undergrad, a skinny Indian boy. *Join us, come, it's already started. We have keropok.*

They are smiling, childishly pleased to encounter a countrywoman so far from home. It makes them feel sophisticated, she imagines, to be in the heart of Manhattan doing something as Singaporean as gathering to watch the parade. She wishes, suddenly, she were the sort of person who'd smile and sit, offer to get a round of coffees, join in the chorus of "Stand Up For Singapore".

Fewer than ten years separate her from them, but they seems to exist in a different universe—more sturdily-built, surer of their place in the world. Looking at them stare expectantly, she knows she ought to say something polite, make an excuse. But something chokes her so instead she smiles tightly, unable to speak, and leaves, almost tripping over a barstool. *Seow*, says one of the boys behind her, not unkindly, and she thinks, *Yes, probably, I probably am a bit crazy.*

The street is full of coffee places, but she walks past the next few, as if the undergrads might come after her, and goes into one that doesn't have a Wi-Fi sign in the window. Her latte arrives with a beach ball etched into the foam—*Happy summer!* beams the barista—and she settles by the window. Every café in the city contains a young woman sunk in thought nursing an overlarge coffee, and no one pays her any attention.

She'd mostly managed to forget what day it was, but now that she's been reminded, it'll niggle at her. If she were back where she came from, she'd be—what? At a barbecue, maybe, and later a pub or something. Certainly not hunched over a computer watching the ceremony. And whom with? People from work, old classmates—it was not very long ago, but she cannot think of any particular friends, just people who happened to be in her vicinity.

It's shaping up to be one of those stridently hot August mornings in New York, when moving anywhere seems slightly too effortful. She has nowhere to be, which is not unusual. This is her existence now. There is probably something she can do that will cause her life to make sense again, somewhere she can go or someone she can speak to, but the idea of extricating herself seems so insurmountable she'd rather not think of it. She has overstayed, and she doesn't even know if she can leave the country without being arrested. She gets by on cash-in-hand work, more or less, but doesn't dare do too much of it. Otherwise, nothing. She shouldn't be drinking expensive coffee. She shouldn't be doing a lot of things.

More blank hours ahead. There is plenty to do that costs nothing in this city, especially in warm weather. She used to sit and read in the library, but that seems increasingly pointless, like studying for an exam that will never come. Lately she has taken to walking in the streets, just anywhere, but preferably here in town. She hates where she lives, its mean proportions, the dirty grey-brown buildings.

Two women come into the shop with their toddlers, which seems like a good moment to leave. Already the anxious young man behind her has stopped tapping into his laptop and is passive-aggressively not moving his chair quite enough for the strollers to get by. She'd rather not get involved in a turf war between young mothers and freelancers. The street is emptier, the remaining pedestrians moving at a less cut-throat pace. Everyone with an office to go to is there by now.

She walks to the end of the block and onto the first

crosswalk to turn green. The day feels vaguely celebratory, though whether from the excess of sunlight or the occasion she cannot say. She passes familiar sights, not so much registering them as enjoying the blur of downtown, the blocky buildings and jostling pavements. The movement calms her. It's good to walk as far and for as long as she can. If she reaches the right level of tiredness, she will be able to sleep properly tonight, easily, without dreams.

Now and then she hears echoes from earlier, *Seow, Come join us,* and the music, that song. If she digs her fingernails into her palms they go away. This is ridiculous, the undergrads have probably forgotten her, and she wouldn't recognise any of them if they met on the subway. But the moment—that is harder to scrub away. An imperfection in the weave that she can't help running her fingers over, again and again.

I need to go home, she mutters, something she says under her breath when she needs to let words slip out. When she looks up, there is a bank of phone booths in front of her. The first one doesn't work and the second is missing its receiver. The third one has a dialling tone—an urban miracle. She taps in her calling card number and then the rest of it.

Her father answers, grunting, *Yes, yes?* When she says nothing, he continues, *Yes? What do you want?* and then *Is it you? It's you, right? Where are you?*

She says, *Happy birthday, Singapore,* and puts the receiver down. She is not a cruel person. Her family should know she is still alive, even if that is all she is prepared to tell them. Perhaps someday—but that is one of those thoughts that never ends well.

A man is standing right behind her. She tries to pass him and almost trips over a leash. He nods apologetically at his small dog, which is sniffing determinedly at the base of the furthest phone booth. *Sorry,* he says. *This is a very interesting neighbourhood for smells. Is your friend called Singapore?*

She isn't sure she's heard correctly. *My friend?*

I couldn't help hearing, on the phone—

Singapore's a country.

Well, I knew that, he is a little flustered, but clearly wishes to be the sort of man who can strike up easy conversations with complete strangers. *It's a, you know, thing. People running around being called America or India. Or China? I'm sure that's a wrestler. Maybe spelled with a "Y".*

It's our National Day, she explains, not sure why she is humouring him, but he seems essentially harmless. *Like your Fourth of July. Independence. There'll be a parade.*

I've never heard anyone say "Happy birthday, America".

She takes a step away and sees the High Line park about a block away. Has she walked that far already? The sun is higher now. They'd probably be almost at the end. The final performances. Some kind of gigantic float. More video. Fireworks. And the hosts shouting—

That's off limits, he says, as if reading her mind. *No dogs on the High Line, for some reason.* As if she'd invited him to join her.

The dog is a shih-tzu, mat-haired and slow-moving, probably fairly old. As she reaches to pet it, it leaps for her hand and releases a dribble of pee down her jeans leg. She looks at the man, appalled, as the animal cheerfully laps at the gap of skin visible where her socks have slipped down.

Sorry, sorry, he gets over-excited, he says, offering her a handkerchief that she makes no move to take. *Really, I'm so—I can't apologise enough. He's an old dog. I'm sure my bladder won't be much better when I'm his age. Would you like to come and get clean? We have wet wipes.* He gestures at an apartment block close by, which makes sense; the dog doesn't look like it would be able to walk very far. She looks closely at him. Flannel shirt and too-tight chinos. The uniform of a different tribe, not someone whose natural habitat is the Meatpacking District.

This is, of course, a terrible idea, which is why she follows him to the building, not offering to help as he struggles to hold the leash and key in the front door code. The interior is musty and in bad need of paint, but a reek of money lingers beneath the stale air. She follows him up to the second floor, keeping her distance from the dog, which leaps from step to step as if each is an individual challenge. She feels she should applaud as it hefts itself onto the landing, panting like a champion.

The flat is an odd diamond shape, a thin hallway opening into a living room with a kitchen bar squished into a corner, narrowing to a tiny bedroom at the back. A board has been roughly tacked onto the window sill to form a crude desk— although you'd have to balance on the back of the sofa to use it. On it is a stack of flyblown paper, a thesaurus, and a typewriter. Not even an electric one.

She raises an eyebrow at him and he confesses, *I'm a writer.* The questions rise naturally to her mouth, *What have you written that I might have—* or *Are you published in—* but she swallows them again. It is patently obvious he is as much of a fuck-up as she. What are the odds that those boxes under the dining table contain unsold novel manuscripts, scrubby thin-papered journals he was once in, rejection letters that agents have taken the time to scribble a personal word or two of encouragement on?

Instead she says, keeping her voice neutral, *I bet you don't find many writers in this neighbourhood.*

I sometimes see Jeffrey Deaver getting milk at the C-store. She continues to stare levelly at him until he confesses, *It's my wife's apartment. I mean, her parents bought it for her. She's at work.* His face suggests the following emotions, in order: reluctance to talk about his wife, realisation that this is what he feels, determination to say something more about his wife because, dammit, why shouldn't he talk about his wife, he has nothing to hide.

And you? she asks.

I teach. He doesn't say where, or what, but there is no need, it explains that he does have a real job, and also why he isn't at it now. He doesn't ask what she does, which suggests he understands too.

They stand for a moment, before he reaches under the sink and starts handing her objects that might be helpful—kitchen roll, laundry soap, stain remover, a sponge. She dabs at the pee stains, almost invisible now, then runs a wet cloth over them. It's probably fine, she can't smell anything and her clothes must pick up much worse from the average subway seat. He looks towards the bedroom and she can tell he is wondering if he should offer her a pair of his wife's trousers. Fortunately, he decides against it.

It's a bit early for a parade, he says conversationally.

She takes a second to work out what he means. *Time difference. It's ten at night in Singapore now.* Smiling to make him feel less stupid, if he'd forgotten, or so she doesn't look like she didn't get the joke, if he were joking.

He reaches down without looking and finds the dog's ears. It must only have one resting position, on the sofa with its head against the middle scatter cushion. There is a moment when she could leave, but it passes and he offers her a drink.

Pressing the icy Coke can against her forehead before opening it, she says, *Can I smoke?* and he replies, *Sure, on the balcony.* She waits a second and adds, *Do you have a cigarette*

I could steal? He meets her eyes and reaches behind a pile of magazines for a packet she's willing to bet the wife doesn't know about. American Spirit.

The balcony is really a fire escape, and can only be reached by clambering over the bed. He goes first, to show how it's done, and she hands him her drink through the window before following. The space outside is tiny, a metal grille with ladders above and below. He opens his own can—diet, she notices—and raises it in a toast. *Happy birthday, Singapore.* She salutes him in return. *It'll be over by now. Everyone's queuing to leave the car park. The performers are scrubbing off their make-up. No more fireworks for another year.*

No fireworks at all?

It's illegal. Maybe a few more at Chinese New Year, but that's it.

Do you miss it?

She lights her cigarette to give herself time to think; he gallantly cups his free hand against the wind. *I don't know. Not really. Not miss, as such.*

But it's been a while since you've—

A little while. It's like if you come from—his accent is hard to place, but she guesses—*Idaho, you might be fond as anything of Idaho, but you don't actually want to live there. Right? So you go away. I've gone away.*

How long? he asks.

She tries not to count, but of course she knows, and

tells him how many months. She could do it to the day, if he wanted more accuracy. *I'm not on the run from the police or anything*—well, not in that way—*You just need to be somewhere else, sometimes.*

Do you want to go back? He has the look of a man who understands the impulse to run away, but has never managed to get very far.

She shrugs. *I don't make plans any more. They've never worked out for me.* It is a good line, and she has practised it. If said with sufficient panache, the right mixture of insouciance and wry humour, it generally prevents further questions.

You'll go back, he says, and she answers, *Maybe.* They leave it there.

They smoke greedily. Like people who don't do it very often, they want to extract as much nicotine as possible with each breath. Not to rule out another one straight after this, but then it might be weeks till the next binge. Her brain blurs pleasantly, and she can see with greater clarity. Actually, the view from the escape is not unpleasant. Three inoffensive brownstones, more metal ladders, the edge of a communal garden. Climbing up two steps and leaning out a little, she can just about see a snatch of the High Line. He is talking somewhat defensively about gentrification, about how the Meatpacking District wasn't nearly so exclusive when he first moved in.

I hope I'm not keeping you from— she bites off the sentence.

He says, *All I have to do is make dinner before Eleanor gets home. It won't take long. I've marinated the tofu. She's a vegetarian.* Again trying not to sound overly deliberate on each mention of the wife, but there isn't a way to do this naturally. Her eyes drift to his fourth finger, which has a ring on it, so.

He lights a new cigarette from the end of the old one, and offers her the packet. She does the same. Being together makes them feel naughty, like children escaping a classroom together. Not the familiar guilt of allowing time to slide irretrievably between her fingers, the choking weight of things undone, things she should do, accumulating day by day and paralysing her all the more. This is illicit, a moment stolen out of normality.

What does Eleanor do? she keeps her voice casual too, but it is like pressing a bruise.

Yoga teacher, he says, straightening his neck and making some kind of adjustment to his spine. *Studio on Bleeker. Big sign on the pavement. You've probably walked by.*

A geyser of wind sweeps between the rows of buildings and pastes stray plastic bags into trees. The heat disappears for a second, but before she can shiver, it is back. *You should have a barbecue out here,* she says.

He pretends to consider this. *Not many guests. A barbecue for two.*

All you need is a grill big enough for two burgers and a sausage.

Bit perverse, he says. Lighting an open fire on a fire escape. Where better?

Speaking of fire—and he reaches towards her, clumsily. Neither of them can move their feet much in this space, and rather than lean back into emptiness she raises her arm in a gesture of protection. The left hand would have meant nothing worse than a splash of Coke to the face, but she has instinctively used her right. *Motherf*— he snaps the word in two, timorously polite even in the face of a cigarette burn to the inside wrist.

Sorry, I was just— she reaches for his hand but he pulls away. *You might have—that was a bit sudden.*

How am I going to explain this? He pulls away his probing finger. There is going to be a scar. A neat, round one.

Deep fry the tofu. Tell her the oil spattered. She is rather pleased with this, but he just glares at her. *Well,* she tries again, somewhat defensively, *You should have asked first.*

Oh, for— He draws a deep breath. *I was just going to*— and he reaches out again. She flinches slightly but forces herself to remain where she is. He rubs her cheek hard and shows her his finger, which is now ashy grey.

The wind must have— she looks at the burnt column dangling off her cigarette, and tips it carefully over the side. *Sorry. I was just*—

Forget it, he says, gruffly.

Do you want me to go now?

Oh, stay, whatever. A day like this. Pee-stained and ash-burned. It's almost biblical.

We could start a new National Day tradition. She smiles at the idea. The undergrads are probably on their way back to their dorm or wherever. Somewhere with chicken curry in the fridge, carefully prepared the night before, and someone's mother's sambal belachan in a jar, duty-free beer, other good things. They'll talk for fifteen minutes about whether this year's parade was better than the last, compare it ironically to the SEA Games opening ceremony, and then move on to something else.

The sun is almost directly overhead now, bleaching the pale stone of his building and illuminating the dancing dust in the bedroom. There is no one out that she can see, no one at all, the alleyway and back gardens are empty, not even a cat, not even a shadow shifting in the windows opposite. She has heard there are abattoirs still amongst the expensive apartment blocks, along with a handful of the packing plants that gave the area its name. Crates of raw flesh, being loaded onto trucks.

He has seen the funny side and is smiling at her now, still nursing his forearm. If anything was going to happen—but of course it never was. She pulls the thought into daylight and laughs at it. He stands before her, schlubby, well-meaning, waiting for the joke to be explained. When she just smiles back at him, he says, *Another Coke?*

Why not? she tips the end of her cigarette into the empty can, adds the previous butt from the window sill, and hands the lot to him. *Never enough caffeine and sugar.*

Whatever gets you through the day. He climbs back into the dinginess of the flat. After a moment, she hears the tap start. He must be running cold water over his arm. She allows herself a dab of guilt—but it was an accident, and he will heal, and who gets to be an adult without visible scars?

She sits on the edge of the platform, her legs dangling over the ladder. Just a little longer, she senses, probably no more than thirty minutes, and it will be time to go, to wander from his home, imagining the buildings she walks past each holding a slaughterhouse, hacking great slabs of animal into manageable chunks, hosing blood off concrete floors. But for a few minutes longer, this can be a place of safety. That's fine, no more is required.

Her day needs remarkably little to gain a shape, to feel less empty at the end. She doesn't know where she'll be tomorrow, or even an hour from now, but she'll be somewhere. The wind fluffs her hair and she tilts her head back, admiring the lacquered blue bowl of the sky, wondrously cloudless, empty apart from the white blaze of the sun. There is nothing else, no fireworks, but it'll do.

National Day

SO WE TAKE a boat to St John's Island because where else can we go, every other place will be crowded and just for one night we want to leave the dormitories, the noise and stink of eight bodies pressed into each small room, just for a few hours we want to escape. Tomorrow is a public holiday so we will start work later than usual, not for our sakes but because the residents complain if construction starts too early while they are still asleep, and the foreman will not say anything if we are back at the site before ten.

Even the ferry terminal is packed, this country is so small that people slosh around and are pushed into each corner. We gather near the bus stop, most of us arriving together from the site but some also from other errands. Antony's girlfriend Veronica has come to see him off, to snatch a few extra minutes with him, and we pretend to look away but still hoot when they kiss. She is embarrassed but smiles gamely, a friendly girl. He waves her onto the bus and strides over to us, a heavy plastic bag tugging at one arm, and we are complete.

We walk past the Formica counters with their bored,

resentful clerks, punished for one infraction or another with a holiday shift. Arul has been before with one of the young things he carts around, and he says they only check tickets on the way back, sometimes you can talk your way out of it, say you lost the stub. We are unsure if this will work for so many of us but Neelish says *Come on, let's take the risk,* and as always we end up listening to him.

There are a few piers with boats going in different directions, some to Indonesia, some closer by, and we follow the lines down, looking for our berth. Most of the passengers are local and Neelish says, *Look, look at them running away from their own birthday party, what kind of people are they, that would never happen back at home.* We try to shush him but he chatters on. Few heads turn to look at us, no one cares what we have to say.

The boat is smaller than we expected, even smaller than a bus, but somehow it contains all of us effortlessly. To the front are young men with plastic fishing boxes and sheaves of gear, and the rest of the space is occupied by teenagers in identical red T-shirts, maybe twenty or thirty of them. We sit on a bench facing back towards the mainland, clearing a space for Jairam's crutches, leaning across each other to talk in our mixture of languages, fractured English and Tamil and Bengali, reaching for whatever words we can find to make ourselves understood. Around us the sailors coil ropes and pull gates shut.

Something slackens and then we are moving, slowly at first and then juddering faster. A cool spray rises as we move past the other boats, then leaving the concrete embrace of the harbour behind for the relief of open water. The sun is not setting yet but the shadows are long, and the tall buildings of the city are at their most attractive, glittering as brightly as the water. They look like beautiful toys, like we could reach out and pluck them from where they stand, the great wheel of the Flyer, the three reaching fingers of the casino, the hard-angled glass and steel of the CBD.

We gape and take pictures if we have cameras on our phones. Mohan points at the lotus flower museum and shouts, *Look, I built that. Ah,* we laugh at him, *but have you ever been inside,* knowing he hasn't, because who could afford that admission fee, and just to look at old porcelain or some foreign painting? Still, we cannot resist doing it too, calling out what we've made, office buildings, skyscraping banks, the Gardens by the Bay with their giant metal trees. *That's mine, I built that.* Despite ourselves, we feel a flicker of something at being a part of this machine, and having operated the cranes and laid the bricks that brought the great city into being.

The boat pulls past Sentosa Cove but it takes us a moment to recognise it, knowing that the houses there cost fifty million dollars at least, as expensive as the moon. From this side they look merely grubby, washed-out pastels behind a scrubby screen of trees, not the palaces we imagined, but then nothing human-made could look well against the blue-green sea, its neat triangular waves in parallel lines as regular as a child's drawing.

Our conversation sputters and we fall into a lull, hypnotised as the mainland slips away and there is space, as if someone has drawn a circle a mile across and placed us alone in its centre. The trip takes less than an hour, and soon we are passing the giant oil drums of Pulau Bukum, the twin green hillocks of the Sisters Islands, and then St John's, its name inscribed in white letters on the slope approaching us, slightly overgrown with grass.

The fishermen are ready to disembark first, leaping onto the jetty before the boat has quite docked, juggling heavy bait boxes and carbon rods, then the teenagers form an orderly line and troop ashore, breaking off in clusters for a photograph under the welcome arch. We are the last to disembark but that is fine, we are not in a hurry and it is easier to manoeuvre Jairam on shore without other people in the way. The crew stand with one foot on the step and the other on land, either side of us, holding the boat in place.

We stand for a moment, telling ourselves this is still Singapore, and yet it is not, this is more like home, so many trees, such silence. A tidy path leads away from the dock and we obediently follow it. There is nothing to the island, it can barely be half a mile in each direction. There is a small hill at one end with a campsite at its peak, where we can see the teenagers shucking their rucksacks, standing in a circle and holding hands. From a safe distance as we amble, a couple of scrawny cats eye us and we wonder what it must be like to come here maybe on a boat, only to find there is nothing, no food, no way back. Mohan, soft-hearted, throws them the remains of a banana from his pocket, but they wait till we are far away before darting up to it.

There are signboards all along the path, green and white and yellow, and Feroz snorts, *These people don't know what to do unless there are black and white words to instruct them, they don't dare wipe their own backsides without government approval.* We stare at the different-sized rectangles, making out the words do not pluck flowers no fishing beyond this point warning no lifeguard on duty.

Looping back to the beach as the sun rests of the top of the tallest buildings on the horizon, we find a place to settle. A floating rope twenty metres from land cordons off the safe swimming area but we wouldn't want to go in anyway, the water here is oil-slicked and gritty, and even the beach is fouled from the ships passing by and the refinery. We sit on towels and sarongs, anything we thought to bring.

Antony pulls from his plastic bag biscuits and fruit and other things that Veronica gets from her ma'am, she says they are given but maybe she just takes them, we don't ask, although the bread is hard and the apples starting to brown and soften, they would just go to waste otherwise. We are grateful because the canteen is closed on holiday evenings and we haven't had dinner yet.

What time do they start? says Feroz, it is his first National Day here and he is as excited as a child. *Soon soon,* we tell him, *eat some fruit, uncle.* We call him that because he is older than us, probably too old to be on a construction site but he lied to the recruiting agent who didn't care as long as he got his cut. What else can he do? It's the last chance for him, scraping together three lakh rupees to cover all the fees, hoping he can stay here long enough to earn that back and make a little more, not much, enough to retire on, hoping he is one of the lucky ones, not like Jairam, not like the ones who come back still in debt, the hollowed-out men every village has.

A wave breaks unexpectedly high and Jairam flinches. We tell him not to worry, we are above the high water mark, and Neelish says, *Yes, but if you're not nice to us we'll roll you down the beach, see if you can swim with one leg.* Neelish has been taking steady nips from a small bottle containing we don't want to ask what, but from the heat rising off him it must be samsu or toddy, something strong. *Eat some bread,* we tell him, *something to soak up the alcohol,* but he barely puts any in his mouth, rolling the rest into little pellets that he flicks into the waves.

What if it rains? says Arul, but it won't, it never rains on National Day. We have heard that they seed the clouds a week before to dry them out. The sky is a clean blue bowl, the thin moon just visible. Even with wind blowing off the sea, the air is blood-warm and heavy around us. *Look*, says Feroz, who has not taken his eyes off the skyline, and he is right, something has started, a hum of thirty thousand people's excitement that we can feel even from here, and then fighter jets buzzing low over the city, apparently just missing half a dozen buildings and disgorging crimson parachutists billowing plumes of coloured smoke behind them. *Showing off,* sniffs Neelish, but even he is unable to take his eyes off the tiny falling figures.

Gouts of music come to us, distorted by the wind, something jaunty with a thumping beat as if we are in a nightclub, and then some kind of military band. *That's the army marching in,* says Sundram, who watched the whole thing on a coffeeshop TV last year. The rest of us have only seen moments, repeats in the news and pictures in the papers the next day. Guns are fired in quick sequence, pop pop pop pop, and there is more cheering.

It is getting dark now. We pile up driftwood and palm leaves and newspapers from the bins, and Antony manages to get the fire going with his lighter, looking a bit shifty as he pulls it out because Veronica's always asking him to quit, he should, cigarettes are so expensive in this city. We don't really have any food to heat up although Arul makes a half-hearted attempt to toast some bread on a stick. The temperature will drop quickly now the sun is gone, and it's comforting to huddle around the glow and warmth.

I recognise this tune, says Feroz, brow furrowed, and we laugh, *Of course you do, uncle, it's that one.* The theme song of this year, it's been played everywhere, on radio and at train stations, something something island sunshine home, syrupy and bland even in these choppy bursts. *Did you know the whole thing costs them seventeen million dollars every year?* says Neelish, who spends his money at Internet cafés looking up facts like these. *Imagine it, so much money for such bad music.*

What would we be doing, on an ordinary night? Sitting on our beds, ignoring the others around us loud on their disposable phones, or lying with heads under our pillows waiting for sleep to take us into another day, a step closer to return. Our few hours here feel stolen, an escape from normality rather than a return to it, as if our other lives have been utterly erased, as if there is nothing left but the scaffolding that we climb up and down all day, our feet never on solid ground.

From up the hill behind us comes the sound of teenagers singing at the camp: *Christ is the Lord of all.* They have just one guitar, equally tuneless, their dirge as deadening as what drifts to us across the water, now back to the band music, pink and green floodlights shooting up into the darkening sky and swaying in time to the beat. Mohan the clown howls like a dog, his impression so unexpectedly accurate that we laugh all over again.

A branch in the fire releases a burst of sparks and we jump. Even with the neon lines of the city back the way we came, there is something primal in the air, as if the noises on the mainland are the crashes and screams of war and we are the only ones who made it out, refugees crouched around our campfire as dark shadows approach. Many-limbed banyan trees stoop above the beach, their tendrils trembling even when the breeze dies down.

What next? says Feroz, but we do not know. Is this one of the years when they bring in the tanks, or will there just be more children dancing? Maybe the tanks are only for when one of the neighbouring countries needs frightening. Not us, our countries are too poor to attack this island, however small it may be, and how could our governments drop bombs on this city when so many of their own citizens are working here?

We stare out to sea as if we can actually follow the show, even though all we can see from here are the leftovers, lasers flicking across neighbouring buildings, helicopters hovering, speedboats churning by close to shore after finishing their turns by the floating platform. Celebrations in our own countries are not so choreographed, so tightly managed. How much fun can they be having? Yet we hear the clapping and stamping from across the water.

Jairam quietly rubs lotion into the stump of his knee, which must be giving him pain, though we have never heard him complain. Antony waves his mobile phone around until he finds reception and has a whispered conversation with Veronica, asking what she's doing and whether she misses him, and the rest of us think of women, girls we left behind in our villages who may or may not be waiting for us, maids or masseuses we encountered here now gone back or departed for countries even further away from their own. We feel not loneliness exactly, but a hollowness in the vicinity of the chest, a helplessness heightened by the wide ocean and starless infinity of the sky above us.

The fishermen are giving up now, walking past with a few tiny specimens dangling from strings. They flung their rods from the causeway over to Lazarus Island, but now are moving back inland. Some seem to live in the kampong huts by the foot of the hill—caretakers? we wonder—and others are at the holiday bungalows, local boys who probably wear G2000 shirts and ties all week and are using the break to flee for a day, to fish and lie in the sun while they can, before responsibility and time thicken their waists and weigh them down. Some look in our direction as they pass but no one speaks to us.

We are getting a little bored, though no one will admit this, but even boredom is a luxury, to be so still that we wish to move again. Some of us look at our phones, others build small sandcastles with plastic cups. The parade doesn't hold much interest for us, at the moment it will be more dancing that we can't see, hundreds of children or civil servants or volunteers running across the stage in neoprene costumes, telling some version of a story that doesn't include us.

Sandaled feet crunch decisively across the sand and then a handful of the teenagers are standing a safe distance away, looking ready to run. A slightly older man, maybe twenty, wearing the same red T-shirt as his charges steps towards us, his voice whiny but trenchant as he says, *What are you doing?*

We are uncertain how to answer, it seems too obvious, so we say nothing, and stare at our feet or at him, and he continues, *You're not allowed to camp here, and you shouldn't light a fire, can't you read the signs?*

You're camping here too, points out Antony, but the man pretends not to hear. He says, *It could be dangerous, I have a whole group of teenagers here, we shouldn't have to put up with this after paying for the use of our campsite, all your illegal activity.*

We say, several of us at once, *We're next to the water, how can it be dangerous, we know what we're doing, do you really think the fire will rush up the hill and burn you?* Not all of us speak English but we try our best to make ourselves understood, waving and pointing to show what we mean. The man's face clenches around the edges and he says, *Okay, I'm asking you guys nicely, please get off this island now.*

This isn't your island, mutters Jairam from the ground, the only one who hasn't stood up, and Arul says, *How, how, you tell me, the last boat for the day has left, you expect us to swim back to land, is it?*

The teenagers have been whispering amongst themselves, and now one of them comes over to the leader, a narrow-faced girl with a wispy fringe and pink plastic glasses, maybe fourteen, her skinny legs awkwardly connecting gym shorts and white ankle socks. The man curves his arm protectively without actually touching her, as if some kind of barrier was needed between us. *Do you need help, Wilson?* she says.

Give me your phone, he says, and when she hands it over he brandishes it in our direction, gripping it so tightly the veins in his forearm stand out. He says, *I can call the police, is that what you want, just one phone call and the police will come and catch you, and you can kiss your work permit goodbye.*

Go ahead and call, says Neelish, walking forward in a manner that is not exactly threatening but certainly not friendly. *Call your police, do you think we're scared, you think they'll come out specially to catch us, everyone's busy at the parade and all, even the coast guard boats are over there, but you can try, I don't think we're so important that they'll come out here just for us, and you're not so important either.*

The girl flinches as if he has smacked her, and the grouped teenagers rustle like they want to say something but do not dare. *You people,* says the man, *you people coming here, we let you into our country and you just take advantage, shouting and making noise and leaving your rubbish anywhere. When will you learn that we have laws here? If you don't like to obey our rules you can just go back home, go away.*

You think you're so clean, we're the ones who clean up after you, sneers Neelish, and we all nod because it is true, we have seen how dirty the streets are each day, how the troops of sweepers clean them just before dawn. We see this and think we are lucky to at least be doing our work, making something that will last, not vanishing unremarked with the sunlight.

We are all motionless now, we have faced people like this before, whenever we try to rest in a park or under a block of flats they come and tell us to leave, not to make the place untidy, not to sit so close to their children. But now there truly is nowhere for us to go, and we wait to see what this man will say. He is a child himself, really, and we pity him as his powerlessness dawns on him and he almost weeps to look so helpless in front of his group. *I warned you,* he says, but the energy has gone out of his voice. He kicks hard at the fire, scattering it, and then almost runs away, his sneakers soot-smeared and his charges flocking after him. Their red T-shirts all have a sturdy cross and the name of a church on the back, marked out in tartrazine yellow.

He's the same age as my son, says Feroz, *I don't think he'd dare to talk to his own father like that.* Neelish drops to his knees and says with an unexpectedly soft voice, *Thambi, are you all right?* And we see Jairam brushing the embers off his stump and saying, *Yes, don't worry.* He wasn't able to get out of the way, of course. He is bleeding a little, the skin on his wound is so fragile still, but fortunately the fire doesn't seem to have touched him.

We use any cloth we can find to clean him up, but not the sea water, it's too dirty. *Those people,* says Mohan as the hymns start again up the hill, but we shush him because there is no point being angry, no point saying anything nor wondering if they will actually call, if the police will be waiting at the docks when we go back. No one rebuilds the fire and it dies out, and then there is only amber light from the lampposts by the path, and the glimmer of the moon on us.

I'm fine, says Jairam again, and Neelish says, *You'd better be, we don't have any way to get you off this island, you'd better be fine.* Jairam is pale from having been in the dormitory for the last four months, on only one-third sick pay and our employer arguing about every step of the medical compensation, and we know that he is a long way from fine, but it serves no purpose to talk about it.

There is a streak of stark white light over the city that turns into a starburst of magenta, and then one of green and yellow. *It's started,* says Feroz without enthusiasm. We sit and watch the fireworks as they spiral and dance in the sky, the reason Neelish persuaded us to come to this island, and the view is as impressive as he promised, but they are not for us, and we see now that we were mistaken in thinking we would be able to enjoy them, they are as foreign and untouchable as the gleaming buildings across the bay, as the teenagers now securely behind the fence of their campsite.

The display goes on for about ten minutes, zigzags and circles and arcs. When the last spray has fizzled away, they play more music. At the parade, people will already be starting to leave in order to beat the crowds and on TV the hosts will be screaming, *Happy birthday, Singapore!* We stay where we are, still sitting, looking at the sky where afterimages linger.

After a long time, Jairam speaks. *In the village I come from,* he says, *every year twenty thirty forty men come to Singapore, they pay so many lakh taka to the agents and disappear, sometimes we never see them again, or they come back and still have debts, but one or two of them will send money home and reappear after many years, so rich, gold teeth and all, the only concrete houses we have belong to people like that, and I thought I could be one of them, someone has to be lucky so why not me, why not take the chance, and now.*

He stops there. Neelish looks at him, Neelish who was beside him when the high-tension steel cable snapped and swung free, whipping through Jairam's leg. We know he still wonders whether he could possibly have moved a little faster, pushed his friend out of the way, maybe flung himself into its path. Nothing more for anyone to say.

And so we remain where we are, one by one lying down on the sand, allowing our eyes to shut. Across the water the celebrations trickle to an end, and even though the lights of the city are as bright as before, something else ends, some energy, as Singaporeans remove themselves and return to their flats, happy to have experienced something positive together and ready for a day of rest, a pause in their busy schedules.

And then we are all sleep, except Neelish, who stands and looks at the sea. Feroz snores raspily and Jairam's bad leg twitches, but they do not wake, and Neelish takes careful steps towards the water, leaving his slippers neatly on a rock before he steps into it, still warm even this late at night. He feels coarse sand and pebbles beneath his feet and the greasy sheen of dirty water against his skin but continues, his trousers wet and then his shirt, kicking his legs when they no longer reach the bottom.

When Neelish reaches the floating barrier he ducks under it and then is in the open sea, slight currents pulling him this way and that, the rolling black surface just visible. From this angle, the city buildings seem even higher, even further, but he continues striking out towards them, not looking back, his face tight and angry as if the water has offended him. Now he thrashes his arms and legs in an inexpert way, his energy pouring into the ocean, propelling him forward a few inches at a time. The waves swell and tumble, but he keeps his head above them. It is just under a mile to the mainland. Perhaps he makes it.

Sophia's Party

FOR WEEKS NOW, they've seen the enormous flag drift through the sky every weekend, held between two rumbling chinooks. Today, the actual event, seems almost an anticlimax. *They spend so much time rehearsing,* says Sophia, pulling trays from the oven. *My mum was in the SOKA contingent a few years back. My god, every single weekend for months she was in that field waving her yellow scarf.*

They just want it to be perfect, says Huixin, who has come round early to help with the preparations. *Everyone will be watching on TV. Even more audience than the Taiwanese serials. Super-embarrassing if someone messes up.*

Nicholas is on the sofa, where he is supposed to remain. Sophia has forbidden him to help—so he won't over-exert himself, she says, but really he suspects because she finds him clumsy, always knocking things over or taking his eyes off saucepans for the crucial ten seconds it takes a sauce to burn. He is trying to be careful anyway, although the operation was months ago and he feels almost normal now.

Instead, it is Huixin who dances round the kitchen on noiseless feet, chopping and rinsing as instructed, now and then returning to her wine glass as delicately as a butterfly to nectar. Their domestic helper Veronica has been given the evening off and instructed not to return before midnight—not just so the guests can be sure it was Sophia who cooked, but also because her windowless room off the kitchen is needed as a staging area. At the moment, chips and crudités line up on the bed in the order in which they'll be served, and a tray of meringue nests on the floor waiting to be filled with fruit and cream.

Sophia's National Day dinner is becoming a bit of a ritual. This is only their third year at this flat, but already her close friends know to keep the date free. Come round around five, no need to bring anything, well, a bottle of wine if you insist. An informal gathering, they sit around reminiscing about the parties they used to have all the time. Nicholas remembers his friendships at the same age, student pubs and too much cider, but Sophia's circle seems to have met in parents' living rooms and dorms instead, centred around food instead of alcohol.

They tried early on to invite both sets of friends, but the guests separated almost immediately, milk and oil, the Singaporeans in a closed ring on the sofa set, and Nicholas's lot on the balcony if they smoked, in the kitchen if they didn't. Sophia later said, *What do you expect, they have nothing in common.* Nicholas could reasonably have retorted that his friends that evening came from at least six different countries—but instead, he quietly agreed they should take turns to curate the guest list for future parties.

Sophia has gone to some effort decorating the flat. Red and white pennants dangle from the ceiling, and a large Merlion balloon, tied to the balcony railing, bobs in the evening breeze. *You said you didn't care about all this,* protested Nicholas as she roamed the flat with her staple gun. She claimed it was all ironic, but he found himself wondering whether Singapore's famously monolithic education system hadn't left its mark on her after all.

It's time, it's time, says Huixin, and darts over to put the television on. The parade doesn't actually start for another hour, but the girls insist on watching every minute of pre-show coverage. A well-groomed woman in a linen jacket sits amongst the white oblongs of a cheap studio set. She says, *Hello, I'm Diana Ser* and the girls chorus, *Hello, Diana!* The stirring music settles down, and Diana's perfectly made-up face shifts and tautens just the right amount to connote excitement as she tells them what's in store this evening.

They angle the screen so they can see it from the kitchen, and return to work, laughing like schoolgirls as they chop onions. *Do you remember,* says Huixin, and wades into a long story about their time in college, sharing an apartment in their sophomore year, adrift without a meal plan for the first time. There are many culinary disaster stories from this phase of their lives. Now Huixin recounts the occasion Sophia's baked mushrooms caused the entire building to be evacuated. *It wasn't my fault at all,* Sophia still insists. *American fire alarms are far too sensitive. They weren't even slightly charred.*

From the sofa, Nicholas throws his eyes out of focus so the thin figures in the kitchen could be college girls still. He often wishes he'd known Sophia then—what he thinks of as her pure state, clean, not yet plated over with experience—although there's little chance she'd have been attracted to him-at-nineteen. Like many Englishmen, he is mildly fascinated by the glamour of American universities, and sometimes imagines Sophia in her tight college sweaters, surrounded by sleek blondes in cut-off jeans and frisky cheerleader outfits.

As if they have burst from his fantasy, a convoy of girls in short skirts tumble onto the field, waving pom-poms in complicated unison. Diana's voice explains that this is a clip of secondary school students rehearsing, as they have been for months, for their part in the event. Pulling back to the studio, she introduces their teacher, an excitable thirtysomething with receding hair and silver-rimmed glasses. *My girls are so enthusiastic,* he says. *I have to shoo them home after practice so their studies don't suffer.*

He is followed by a succession of behind-the-scenes volunteers, the make-up artists, the puppet-makers, the choreographers, some shown in their workshops or studios, others sharing Diana's sofa, explaining what the occasion means to them, how they have worked as a team, as a family to achieve this. Nicholas is as patriotic as the next man, but he finds such displays discomfiting, mawkish. Still, the broadcast is handsomely produced, stirring images of young people rehearsing dance steps against the setting sun, of an old man correcting his granddaughter's fingering on the sitar.

And in between, the camera pulls back to the seating stand, where rows of people wave balloons, oddly blank-faced but apparently determined to have a good time. Tickets are free, but must be balloted for months in advance, and every year there are rumours of them changing hands on Gumtree or Craigslist for hundreds of dollars. Can this really be? But people will buy anything these days.

The government arrives. Huixin cheers, her little flag held high. The Ministers parade in, all in dumpy red-and-white polo shirts and slacks, what Sophia calls "tragic-casual". They wave at the crowd and look around for their seats. The Prime Minister is in an odd confection, vermillion triangles slashed across with cream. *He's probably wearing some local fashion designer,* says Huixin knowingly. *Like Michelle Obama.*

And now, the announcer's voice booms across the field, *it's the moment we've all been waiting for. Ladies and gentlemen, the Red Lions!* A trio of fighter jets appears over the city. As they zoom closer, the doorbell rings. *Not during the Red Lions,* screeches Sophia, her eyes glued to the screen as she walks backwards to the front door. She lets in two people and shushes them, *Red Lions, shh.* One by one, men in scarlet jumpsuits are disgorged from the planes and tumble gracefully onto the narrow strip of grass. They all land feet first, running from momentum, somehow graceful even while trailing yards of silk behind them.

I don't know why you get so excited, it's exactly the same every year, says Huixin, when the last parachutist has made his drop.

But just imagine if one year someone landed in the wrong place or something, wouldn't you want to see it?

Huixin snorts. *That will never happen. Nothing ever goes wrong on National Day. Do you know, they even seed the clouds the week before so it won't rain on the big day?*

Hi, says one of the new guests. *I'm Brian.* His round, pleasant face is slightly pitted from acne. He holds a firm hand out to Nicholas. *Oh, sorry, don't you guys know each other?* says Sophia, stricken, as if she has failed some kind of test. No—Nicholas has met the wife, Joy, several times, but this is the first time Brian is joining her. *Usually only one of us can come out, because of the baby,* he explains earnestly, *but tonight my mother volunteered to take care of her.*

Can we help? says Joy, but Sophia waves her away, already on her way back to the kitchen. *It's under control.* She mashes olives into tapenade while Huixin hollows out little cucumber boats ready to be filled. On the counter in front of them sit a row of cookbooks, Jamie Oliver and River Cottage and Mrs Violet Oon, all open to the right pages

and covered in meticulously detailed post-it notes. Sophia's
dinner parties are run with the military precision of a parade,
and she has worked out the timing of each dish with breaks
in the schedule for her favourite bits of the show.

Marooned on the sofa with Brian and Joy, Nicholas is
saved from the need for conversation by the next item, the
army marching in. *This is Second Armour Brigade,* bellows
the announcer. *This is Sixth Division Engineers.* Watching
from her perch, Diana says how proud she is of these brave
men, defending our nation. *The propaganda parade,* Nicholas
snorts, then wonders if he has made a faux pas from the
unyielding faces of the other two. Later, Sophia will inform
him that Brian is fiercely loyal to his unit from National
Service, and is perennially disappointed not to be chosen for
the parade as part of his reservist duties.

With the army installed in rectangular blocks across the
field, the choir file into their tiered stand. A tiny girl, perhaps
eight, steps forward and begins the verse, a capella for a few
bars before the band gently comes in underneath her. The
other singers join her for the chorus. It is that song, the
theme song of the year that has been playing everywhere,
even spewing out of the new video-screen bus stop ads, a
blandly memorable tune. *This light is mine, this island light,*
warbles Huixin, a semi-tone flatter than the choir. *Pace
yourself,* advises Sophia. *We'll be hearing it a few times tonight.*

The captain shouts a command in Malay and the troops

begin moving again. The camera picks out their firm arms, their rigid faces, and Nicholas feels his crisp European disdain of military matters melting around the edges. He thinks of himself as a pacifist, above the tinsel pomp of soldiers on parade, yet there is something seductively virile about these men in uniform, the regularity of them.

Part of this is chagrin at his own body letting him down. He is back at work now, and even though nobody mentions the operation, there is a definite sense of being on light duties, even sidelined. The banking world is not one to tolerate weakness, and physical deficiency of any kind receives minimal sympathy. Like a slowly bleeding wound, it only encourages the sharks to circle.

The president appears, in a grey suit, white hair slicked back. He stands awkwardly as the National Anthem plays and the flag is raised. Nicholas looks around the flat, but none of the others show signs of rising to their feet, standing to attention. The parade commander raises a sword to his face, almost kissing it, and shouts, *Mr President, the parade is form up ready for inspection, SIR.* Nicholas winces at the bad grammar, before reminding himself not to be such a neo-colonialist.

For a moment, it is like being in a military dictatorship. The president, in a follow-spot, walks at a stately pace down the rows of soldiers, who hold their rifles high, bayonets unsheathed. In the bay beyond the floating stage, gunboats fire into the air. On the giant screens at the back of the stage, a montage plays, telling the story of Singapore's army, boys leaving for National Service, fathers and sons serving in the same unit.

When the president has finished his slow progress, constantly stopping to examine an insignia or share a few words with a second sergeant, he is escorted back to his seat. More orders are shouted, and a line of men raise their rifles into the air and fire, one after another, a string of pops and explosions. Nicholas feels a shiver of unease, more at the cheers of the crowd than the noise—how can anyone listen to rifles being cocked and fired without even a whisper of terror? But the other faces in the room are rapt, Brian cocking a finger as if he too held a firearm.

Then the troops are marching off the field and just like that, the show of force is over. It is dusk by now, and illuminated screens slide onto the stage while neon-bright lasers slice through the darkening sky. Sophia skips in from the kitchen with a tray of Doritos and dip, and when the doorbell goes, she pirouettes to answer it. The music shifts from Sousa marches to a soupy mix of national songs as the performers begin to file on, all brightly made-up in neoprene costumes.

Sophia comes back in with a man Nicholas vaguely recognises. *Calvin,* says Joy reproachfully. *Why so late? You missed the whole parade.* Calvin sullenly mutters something about having too much work, even on a supposed public holiday, and the constant persecution of being a civil servant. *We're civil servants too,* says Joy, but he slaps away her comment. *You're teachers, that's not the same thing.*

At least you're in time to catch the show, says Brian, pushing the chips in his direction. He grunts and scoops up a handful. A couple of days from now, Nicholas will finally feel strong enough to ask his wife why on earth she invited this person, and she will reply that she felt sorry for him; he doesn't get on with his family and for some reason he's been single forever.

On the stage, a handful of schoolchildren are performing a sketch, over-enunciating every word as they've been trained to. Something about home being where they belong. As is expected, they are scrupulously diverse—both boys and girls, two Chinese, one Malay, one Indian, and an indeterminate one who is probably Eurasian. *Come quickly, Soph, you're missing the opening,* calls Joy, and Huixin darts out with cocktail sausages and napkins. *Almost done,* she says breathlessly.

By the time the dancing starts, the girls have laid a feast out on the coffee table. It is all finger food, easy to eat without taking your eyes off the screen. They are all now ranged around the TV set, on the sofa and pouffes and armrests, picking at dinner, watching the contingents of adults run out to surround the children, wheeling in and out of each other, droning their song. As a giant silk orchid, the national flower, blossoms behind them, they raise their arms to it. Huixin and Joy join in the chorus.

The number lasts no more than ten minutes, but by the end of it the mood of the evening has been quite transformed. Choreography on such a massive scale must take no less co-ordination than the military parade, Nicholas knows—indeed, he read somewhere that the army helps train the schoolchildren in learning the dance steps—but this is sweetly unthreatening, soft and gauzy. Even Sophia, global traveller that she is, looks moved by the display. This is a school concert amped up on a massive scale, Nicholas tells himself, but even then it is hard to resist the shameless manipulation of expertly-designed proselytising.

As the first set of performers leave, the screen brightens into another montage, more national songs, more faces saying what this country means to them. *More advertising,* laughs Huixin, and Joy says, *Of course, this whole thing is an advertisement for the country.* It is easy to mock the cheap sentimentality of this video, and Nicholas joins in, *They'd better make sure they're targeting the right audience. Maybe nobody wants to buy what they have.*

If you don't like it, feel free to leave, says Calvin sourly, and there is a frozen moment before everyone leaps in. *He didn't mean it like that,* says Sophia. At the same time, Huixin wades in with something about how they don't have National Day celebrations in Britain so Nicholas doesn't understand what this is all about, he didn't mean to be offensive. They are apologising on his behalf rather than defending him, Nicholas notices, not saying anything himself. There are moments when he wonders how much he will ever fit into this country, how much of himself he will have to slough off before he can glide through these occasions without friction.

Do we need to leave food for anyone? says Joy in a transparent attempt to change the subject—there is no danger that they will run out, the girls have prepared enough for at least double the number. *Karen's at Brewerkz, she said maybe she'll come later,* says Sophia, which they all know means she won't. This happens every year, Karen promising herself to three or four parties and sending drunken texts through the evening deferring her arrival at each.

The next segments of the show are more of the same, hundreds of volunteers moving in formation to make a lion's head, the shape of the island, a glowing torch, in between fluttering their props—fans, lanterns, trailing ribbons—so ripples quiver over the mass of individuals. Now and then there is a theatrical coup. Blue parachute silk glides suddenly over the space, white sails popping up as if from nowhere. *To depict the difficult journeys our immigrant forefathers undertook to arrive here,* explains the emcee. As she speaks, the bay glows suddenly as dozens of sampans put on their lights and unfurl sails, bobbing towards the floating stage.

Eat some more, says Sophia, returning from the kitchen

with a tray of spiced chicken wings and roquefort arancini, *but save room for dessert.* Nicholas she nudges with the heel of her hand and mouths, *Pills.* It has become part of the ritual of every meal time, the ration of immuno-suppressants that keeps him alive, the thrice-daily reminder that he is not a whole man. The others look away politely as he rattles a multi-coloured stream from his pill-container. Sophia brings him a glass of water.

Everyone must now be sated, but they continue picking at the savoury mouthfuls while the TV blares more music, more commentary. *Remember at uni, your mum would record the parade and post it to us—and we thought it was so high-tech because she burnt it to a CD-ROM, not videotape.* Joy laughs at the memory, and Brian chips in. *Yeah, nowadays the kids are probably live-streaming it on Youtube.*

Clear, sinuous erhu music gives way to a bespectacled schoolboy rapping somewhat self-consciously, then bhangra drums pick up this beat and draw in some weepy gamelan. *So many different cultures coming together seamlessly,* proclaims the announcer, sounding emotional. *That sums up everything that's special about Singapore.*

More schoolchildren bubble onto the stage. Or the same ones in different costumes? There seems to be an inexhaustible supply. They spread into three groups—Chinese fan dancers in pink and blue, Malay girls doing the ronggeng in green, and an Indian kathak group in golden saris. *Multi-racialism,*

Singapore style, rejoices the announcer. *Multi-racial if you're Chinese, Malay or Indian,* says Joy, who is some complicated blend of Portuguese, Javanese and Thai, and frequently complains that the only category available to her on forms is "Other". There isn't a pigeonhole for Nicholas either, but he says nothing.

And all across the island, in tiny flats like this, people are sprawled before their TV sets, absorbing the entertainment provided for them, imbibing the messages, overt or not— though none particularly subtle—and feeling stirrings of patriotism and belonging. *Can it be that simple?* wonders Nicholas. But it must work at some level. All the Singaporeans in this room have spent a few years abroad, and all have returned, the idea of greener pastures seeming not to occur to them at all.

So Huixin, are you seeing anyone these days? Calvin has leaned across the table and is rather grotesquely allowing his hand to graze her wrist, his voice probably louder than he means it to be. She shakes her head firmly, but he doesn't seem to see. *I thought maybe we could go for a drink, I mean, not all of us, just the two—* He breaks off as he realises they are all looking. Did he think he could slide this in unnoticed under the performance music?

Huixin jumps up. *Excuse me.* And she is efficiently stacking dishes, brushing crumbs from the table. Sophia, too, begins whisking glasses into the kitchen. Too late, Nicholas notices the four empty beer bottles at Calvin's feet, and a fifth in his hand. He does not look like a man who can hold his liquor.

I'll help, says Joy gracefully, and heads to the kitchen too. The girls huddle tactfully in the far corner, where they cannot be seen. Calvin looks crestfallen, mumbling that he hadn't meant to upset anyone. *Let it go, man,* says Brian. *This always happens,* says Calvin, shaking his head. *I'm a nice guy, I asked nicely, but they're never interested in nice guys.* Nicholas can think of nothing to say, and sits stiffly as Brian talks about waiting for the right person to come along.

The awkwardness threatens one minute to take over the evening, and the next is dispelled entirely as Huixin comes running into the living room. *Fireworks!* she cries, and sure enough they are bursting ripely over the night sky, pink chalky streaks, green whirligigs and yellow stars, fizzling on the TV screen at the same time as the emcee shouts *Happy birthday, Singapore!* and the spectators wave the giant inflatable lions they've been given.

They crowd onto the narrow balcony, childishly excited by the spectacle. Outside the air-conditioning, the night air is heavy and humid. Brian raises his glass in a toast and those who brought their drinks out join him. *Happy National Day,* says Sophia, and unexpectedly hugs Nicholas. She is trembling slightly, from excitement or stray emotion or the stress of the evening.

Back inside, she wheels out a retro hostess trolley with an

array of desserts: red agar-agar, profiteroles, cupcakes with lion heads stamped into their icing. The parade is winding down after the climax of the pyrotechnics. When the camera pans over the crowd, some of them are already heading for the exits, trying to beat the car park rush. All the performers have gathered on the field and are once again singing that song.

By the time the credits roll, the party has entered a comfortable state of vegetative equilibrium, the sense that all rough edges have been smoothed out, at least for tonight, and they can marinate in one another's presence. Sophia proudly produces a variety of caffeinated beverages from their new Nespresso machine, the stimulating effect of coffee seeming to keep people barely awake, rather than actually energising them.

Nicholas finds his mind drifting towards sleep, and when he returns, Joy is, for some reason, telling the story of how she met Brian. He looks nervously at Calvin in case coupledom is a sensitive point still, but Calvin seems lulled into gentle stasis, the earlier episode smoothed away, and is looking at them as if they are a distant story, nothing to do with him. It is not, in any case, a particularly riveting tale—they were introduced by mutual friends, and later discovered they'd trained as teachers in the same batch but never actually met. And then the marriage, the HDB flat and the baby.

And you and Nicholas? says Huixin. *You know the story,* protests Sophia, but this happens all the time, especially after a few drinks. Huixin wanting to hear it again, like a child, what she calls the fairy tale of their marriage.

They are practiced at this, and Nicholas knows when he is expected to chip in, when to laugh or contradict her on trivial details or nod emphatically. *He actually left me,* she is saying. *He wanted to go back to London. I was heartbroken, wasn't I, dear?*

He nods, sombrely. *You begged me to stay—*

Asked you to stay—

But I wouldn't. I'd had enough—this country, it suffocates you, if you aren't careful. So I went away—

But then... Sophia threads her arm through his, rests her head on his shoulder. *As soon as he got to Heathrow, the minute he touched down, he realised he'd made a terrible mistake. That's what he said to me, a terrible mistake. And without even unpacking his bags, he went straight to the British Airways counter and bought a ticket back to Singapore.*

Nicholas smiles at the top of her head. It actually took him six months to acknowledge that he missed her, and then another two to persuade her to take him back. Still, he must admit that her version of events is more engaging. He wonders if she has by now convinced herself of it. *I came back for her,* he thinks. *She pulled me back to this place.*

So romantic, Joy is saying. *I wish someone would do that for me.*

What, leave you and come back again? Brian, raucous. *I can do that, the first part anyway, I might forget to come back.*

Idiot. I mean, give up everything for me.

What makes you think he's given up anything? Look at him.
What else does he need?

And Nicholas, looking at his tasteful flat, his beautiful
wife, honestly believes at this moment that he does have
everything he needs. Some version of health, and more
than enough money to keep them from starvation. Here
they are, and the story is as good an organising principle
as any to make sense of their lives. He wonders sometimes
how long they will stay in this country, and how long
they will remain together. At least hearing Sophia talk so
brightly about their early days, how they began, makes him
feel momentarily hopeful.

Leaning back, looking companionably at his wife's friends,
Nicholas sinks into a warm fog of alcohol and something
like contentment. His mind fills with the memory of himself
returning, the prodigal, not much younger than now but
entirely different. The day he stood, indecisive, in the great
bronze hall of Changi Terminal 2, wondering if this was right
or yet another mistake. Stiff currents of air-conditioning
swirled around his body and muffled announcements called
out other arrivals. His luggage slumped on a trolley next to
him, cumbersome, everything he owned. What next? What
next for him?

A second before the fear became overwhelming, he

felt a change in temperature and sensed rather than heard
her footstep. This is what's next, he thought. This is the
next moment. Breath came back into his body. His mind
gleaming, the air thick around him, Nicholas steadied
himself and turned to see, striding towards him—Sophia,
her eyes wet, her arms wide with welcome.

About the Author

Jeremy Tiang's writing has appeared in *The Guardian, Esquire (Singapore), Asia Literary Review, Brooklyn Rail, Drunken Boat, Meanjin, Ambit, Quarterly Literary Review Singapore* and the first two volumes of *The Epigram Book of Best New Singaporean Short Stories*. He won the Golden Point Award in 2009 and has been shortlisted for the *Iowa Review* Award and *American Short Fiction* Prize. He has also translated more than ten books from the Chinese, including work by You Jin, Wong Yoon Wah, Yeng Pway Ngon, Yan Geling and Zhang Yueran, and has been awarded translation grants from PEN American Center, the National Endowment for the Arts (USA) and the National Museum of Taiwanese Literature. Jeremy's plays include *The Last Days of Limehouse* (Yellow Earth, London), *Floating Bones* (The Arts House; translations of Han Lao Da and Quah Sy Ren one-acts) and *A Dream of Red Pavilions* (Pan Asian Rep, NYC; adapted from the novel by Cao Xueqin). He lives in New York City.

Acknowledgements

MUCH OF THIS book grew out of my time at various writing residencies, for which I thank all at the University of Iowa's International Writing Program (including but not limited to Christopher Merrill, Hualing Nieh Engle, Nataša Durovicová, Mary and Peter Nazareth, Hugh Ferrer, Joe Tiefenthaler, Kecia Lynn, Nate Brown and Kelly Bedeian), Kulturverein Mecklenburg Inspiriert at Kühlungsborn (particularly Familie Kurbjuhn and all at Hotel Polar-Stern for their generous hospitality), Sangam House (Arshia Sattar, Rahul Soni and DW Gibson) and the Chennai Mathematical Institute (K Srilata, KV Subrahmanyam and Madhavan Mukund).

I am also grateful to the journals that have published these stories individually, and the editors who made them so much better along the way: Martin Alexander at the *Asia Literary Review*, Briony Bax at *Ambit*, Yeow Kai Chai at *QLRS*, Zora Sanders at *Meanjin*, Hande Zapsu Watt at *The Istanbul Review*, Ravi Shankar and Alvin Pang at *Drunken Boat*, Andrew Lloyd-Jones, Dan Coxon and Eric Akoto at *Litro*, and Joel Toledo at the *Philippines Free Press*. Also, thanks to Dorothy Tse for her fine translation of "Stray" into Chinese.

The travel that provided the raw material for these stories could not have taken place without the help of many friends, including: Glynne Steele for bringing me to Zurich, Susan Sturton and Maarten Felix for their hospitality in Trondheim, Jacqui Harrison for driving all the way to Prora, Zhang Yueran for my time in Beijing, Nicole St Martin and Michael Bradley for their hospitality in Toronto, Tim Luscombe for the flat in Bangkok, and Caroline Lena Olsson for the Meatpacking flat.

I also used as reference points Jonathan Mirsky's "China's Death-Row Reality Show" (*New York Review of Books*) and Ethan Gutmann's "The Xinjiang Procedure" (*The Weekly Standard*) for "Sophia's Aunt", the KdF Museum Prora for "Schwellenangst", and the interviews with migrant workers at Transient Workers Count Too for "National Day".

And finally my agent Karolina Sutton, my editor Jason Erik Lundberg, Edmund Wee and all at Epigram Books.

Some of these stories were originally published, in slightly different form, as follows:

"Sophia's Honeymoon" in *Istanbul Review* (Feb 2013), *The Sangam House Reader*, (Nov 2013) and *Singapore Poetry* (Apr 2014); "Schwellenangst" in *Litro* no. 125 (May 2013) and *Transatlantic: The Litro Anthology* (Oct 2014); "Sophia's Aunt" as "Beijing Hospital" in *Asia Literary Review* no. 27 (Spring 2015); "Toronto" in *Meanjin* (Jan 2014) and *The Epigram Books Collection of Best New Singaporean Short Stories: Volume Two* (Oct 2015); "Harmonious Residences" in *Quarterly Literary Review Singapore* vol. 10 no. 1 (Jan 2011) and *The Epigram Books Collection of Best New Singaporean Short Stories: Volume One* (Oct 2013); "Stray" in *Philippines Free Press* (Nov 2010) and *Fleurs des Lettres* (May 2012, translated into Chinese by Dorothy Tse); "Meatpacking" in *Drunken Boat* no. 21, Union Folio (Apr 2015); "National Day" in *Ambit* no. 216 (Spring 2014) and *UNION: 15 Years of Drunken Boat, 50 Years of Writing From Singapore* (Sep 2015); "Sophia's Party" in *Quarterly Literary Review Singapore* vol. 12 no. 4 (Oct 2013).

"Trondheim" won the 2009 Golden Point Award for English Fiction, and appeared on the National Arts Council's website. "Tick" is original to this collection.